W9-BRN-670

Philadelphia
Cream Cheese

Collection

pil
Publications International Ltd.

Publications International Ltd.

Microwave Cooking: Microwave ovens vary in wattage. Use the cooking times as guidelines and check for doneness before adding more time.

Preparation/Cooking Times: Preparation times are based on the approximate amount of time required to assemble the recipe before cooking, baking, chilling or serving. These times include preparation steps such as measuring, chopping and mixing. The fact that some preparations and cooking can be done simultaneously is taken into account. Preparation of optional ingredients and serving suggestions is not included.

38

132

98

Easy Appetizers

Baked Cream Cheese Appetizer

Prep Time: 10 minutes   *Bake Time:* 18 minutes

1 can (4 ounces) refrigerated crescent dinner rolls
1 package (8 ounces) PHILADELPHIA® Cream Cheese
½ teaspoon dill weed
1 egg white, beaten

UNROLL dough on lightly greased cookie sheet; firmly press perforations together to form 12×4-inch rectangle.

SPRINKLE cream cheese with dill; lightly press dill into cream cheese. Place cream cheese, dill-side up, in center of dough. Bring edges of dough up over cream cheese; press edges of dough together to seal, completely enclosing cream cheese. Brush with egg white.

BAKE at 350°F for 15 to 18 minutes or until lightly browned. Serve with NABISCO® Crackers, French bread or fresh fruit slices.   ***Makes 8 servings***

Great Substitutes: Substitute combined ½ teaspoon dried rosemary leaves, crushed, and ½ teaspoon paprika for the dill weed.

Black Bean Spirals

Prep Time: 15 minutes plus refrigerating

- 1 can (15 ounces) black beans, rinsed, drained
- 6 flour tortillas (10-inch)
- 1 package (8 ounces) PHILADELPHIA® Cream Cheese, softened
- 1 cup KRAFT® Shredded Cheddar *or* Monterey Jack Cheese
- ½ cup BREAKSTONE'S® or KNUDSEN® Sour Cream
- ¼ teaspoon onion salt
- TACO BELL® HOME ORIGINALS® Thick 'N Chunky Salsa

PLACE beans in food processor container fitted with steel blade or blender container; cover. Process until smooth. Spread layer of beans on each tortilla.

PLACE cheeses, sour cream and onion salt in food processor container fitted with steel blade or blender container; cover. Process until smooth. Spread cheese mixture over beans.

ROLL tortillas up tightly. Refrigerate 30 minutes. Cut into ½-inch slices. Serve with TACO BELL® HOME ORIGINALS® Thick 'N Chunky Salsa.   *Makes 20 servings*

Great Substitute: Substitute 1 can (16 ounces) TACO BELL® HOME ORIGINALS® Refried Beans for pureed black beans.

Philadelphia® Crabmeat Spread

Prep Time: 5 minutes

- 1 package (8 ounces) PHILADELPHIA® Cream Cheese, softened
- ¼ cup cocktail sauce
- 1 package (8 ounces) imitation crabmeat *or* 1 package (6 ounces) frozen cooked tiny shrimp, thawed, drained

SPREAD cream cheese on serving plate.

POUR cocktail sauce over cream cheese; top with imitation crabmeat. Serve with crackers or cocktail rye bread slices.   *Makes 10 servings*

Philadelphia® Pesto Christmas Tree

Prep Time: 5 minutes

   1 package (8 ounces) PHILADELPHIA® Cream Cheese
   ⅓ cup DI GIORNO® Basil Pesto Sauce
    Cinnamon stick

CUT cream cheese in half diagonally. Place triangles together to form Christmas tree shape on serving plate.

TOP with pesto. Insert cinnamon stick at to make trunk shape. Serve with NABISCO® Crackers.   *Makes 12 servings*

Special Extra: Use chopped red pepper as "ornaments" to decorate tree.

Bacon Appetizer Crescents

Prep Time: 30 minutes   *Bake Time:* 15 minutes

   1 package (8 ounces) PHILADELPHIA® Cream Cheese, softened
   ½ cup OSCAR MAYER® Bacon Bits *or* 8 slices OSCAR MAYER® Bacon,
     crisply cooked, crumbled
   ⅓ cup KRAFT® 100% Grated Parmesan Cheese
   ¼ cup thinly sliced green onions
   1 tablespoon milk
   2 cans (8 ounces each) refrigerated crescent dinner rolls
    Poppy seed (optional)

MIX cream cheese, bacon bits, Parmesan cheese, onions and milk until well blended.

SEPARATE dough into 8 rectangles; firmly press perforations together to seal. Spread each rectangle with 2 rounded tablespoonfuls cream cheese mixture.

CUT each rectangle in half diagonally; repeat with opposite corners. Cut in half crosswise to form 6 triangles. Roll up triangles, starting at short ends. Place on ungreased cookie sheets. Sprinkle with poppy seed.

BAKE at 375°F for 12 to 15 minutes or until golden brown. Serve immediately.
        Makes 4 dozen

Savory Bruschetta

Prep Time: 15 minutes   *Bake Time:* 10 minutes

¼ **cup olive oil**
1 **clove garlic, minced**
1 **loaf (1 pound) French bread, cut in half lengthwise**
1 **package (8 ounces) PHILADELPHIA® Cream Cheese, softened**
3 **tablespoons KRAFT® 100% Grated Parmesan Cheese**
2 **tablespoons chopped pitted Niçoise olives**
1 **cup chopped plum tomatoes**
   Fresh basil leaves

MIX oil and garlic; spread on cut surfaces of bread. Bake at 400°F for 8 to 10 minutes or until toasted. Cool.

MIX cream cheese and Parmesan cheese with electric mixer on medium speed until blended. Stir in olives. Spread on cooled bread halves.

TOP with tomatoes and basil leaves. Cut into slices.   *Makes 2 dozen*

Chunky Potato Soup

Prep Time: 15 minutes   *Cook Time:* 25 minutes

6 **slices OSCAR MAYER® Bacon, chopped**
1 **large leek, chopped** *or* ½ **cup chopped green onions**
1 **can (13¾ ounces) chicken broth**
1 **cup milk**
1 **package (8 ounces) PHILADELPHIA® Cream Cheese, cubed**
4 **cups diced peeled potatoes**

COOK bacon in 5-quart Dutch oven or saucepot on medium heat until crisp, turning frequently. Drain bacon, reserving 2 tablespoons drippings in Dutch oven. Set bacon aside.

ADD leek to reserved 2 tablespoons drippings in Dutch oven; cook and stir 5 minutes or until tender. Stir in broth, milk and cream cheese; stir on low heat until cream cheese is melted.

ADD potatoes; cook on low heat 20 to 25 minutes or until potatoes are tender, stirring occasionally.   *Makes 6 (1-cup) servings*

Southwestern Cheesecake

Prep Time: 20 minutes plus refrigerating   *Bake Time:* 30 minutes

1 cup finely crushed tortilla chips
3 tablespoons butter *or* margarine, melted
2 packages (8 ounces) PHILADELPHIA® Cream Cheese, softened
2 eggs
1 package (8 ounces) KRAFT® Shredded Colby/Monterey Jack Cheese
1 (4-ounce) can chopped green chilies, drained
1 cup BREAKSTONE'S® *or* KNUDSEN® Sour Cream
1 cup chopped yellow *or* orange bell pepper
½ cup green onion slices
⅓ cup chopped tomatoes
¼ cup sliced pitted ripe olives

MIX chips and butter in small bowl; press onto bottom of 9-inch springform pan. Bake at 325°F for 15 minutes.

BEAT cream cheese and eggs at medium speed with electric mixer until well blended. Mix in shredded cheese and chilies; pour over crust. Bake for 30 minutes.

SPREAD sour cream over cheesecake. Loosen cake from rim of pan; cool before removing rim of pan. Chill.

TOP with remaining ingredients just before serving.

Makes 16 to 20 appetizer servings

Note: To make an attractive design on top of this cheesecake, cut three diamonds out of paper. Place on top of cheesecake. Place green onion slices around diamonds. Remove cutouts; fill in with bell peppers. Add a strip of tomatoes down the center. Garnish with olives.

Corned Beef & Swiss Appetizers

Prep Time: 20 minutes   *Broil Time:* 3 minutes

   1 package (8 ounces) PHILADELPHIA® Cream Cheese, softened
   2 teaspoons Grey Poupon® Dijon Mustard
  ¼ pound corned beef, chopped
  ½ cup (2 ounces) KRAFT® Shredded Swiss Cheese
   2 tablespoons chopped green onion
 36 slices cocktail rye bread, toasted

MIX cream cheese and mustard with electric mixer on medium speed until smooth.

BLEND in meat, Swiss cheese and onion. Spread on toast slices. Place on cookie sheet.

BROIL 2 to 3 minutes or until lightly browned.   *Makes 3 dozen*

To Make Ahead: Prepare as directed except for broiling. Place on cookie sheet. Freeze 1 hour or until firm. Place in freezer-safe zipper-style plastic bags. Freeze up to 1 month. When ready to serve, thaw 10 minutes. Broil as directed.

Deviled Vegetable Crab Spread

Prep Time: 30 minutes   *Cook Time:* 20 minutes

   1 package (8 ounces) PHILADELPHIA® Cream Cheese, softened
  ¼ cup GREY POUPON® Dijon Mustard
   2 tablespoons milk
 12 PREMIUM® Crackers (any variety), finely crushed (½ cup crumbs)
   1 (6-ounce) can crabmeat or tuna, drained and flaked
  ¼ cup chopped green onions
  ¼ cup chopped red bell pepper
    Additional PREMIUM® Crackers

BEAT cream cheese in small bowl with electric mixer at medium speed until smooth; add mustard and milk, beating until well blended.

ADD cracker crumbs, crabmeat or tuna, green onions and bell pepper. Place in greased 8-inch pie plate or small baking dish.

BAKE at 350°F for 20 minutes or until golden brown and hot. Serve as a spread with crackers.   *Makes about 2⅓ cups*

Party Cheese Wreath

Prep Time: 15 minutes plus refrigerating

2 packages (8 ounces each) PHILADELPHIA® Cream Cheese, softened
1 package (8 ounces) KRAFT® Shredded Sharp Cheddar Cheese
1 tablespoon *each* chopped red bell pepper and finely chopped onion
2 teaspoons Worcestershire sauce
1 teaspoon lemon juice
Dash ground red pepper

MIX cream cheese and cheddar cheese with electric mixer on medium speed until well blended.

BLEND in remaining ingredients. Refrigerate several hours or overnight.

PLACE drinking glass in center of serving platter. Drop round tablespoonfuls of mixture around glass, just touching outer edge of glass to form ring; smooth with spatula. Remove glass. Garnish with chopped fresh parsley and chopped red pepper. Serve with NABISCO® Crackers. ***Makes 12 servings***

Special Extra: Shape cream cheese mixture into 1-inch balls. Roll in light rye bread crumbs or dark pumpernickel bread crumbs.

Pecan Cheese Ball

Prep Time: 15 minutes *Chill Time:* 1 hour

1 package (8 ounces) PHILADELPHIA® Cream Cheese, softened
1 cup KRAFT® Shredded Cheddar Cheese (4 ounces)
½ cup crumbled blue cheese (4 ounces)
½ cup PLANTERS® Pecans, chopped
RITZ® Crackers

BLEND cheeses in medium bowl with electric mixer at medium speed.

SHAPE cheese mixture into ball; roll in pecans. Refrigerate for at least 1 hour.

SERVE as spread with crackers. ***Makes 2 cups spread***

Roasted Red Pepper Pesto Cheesecake

Prep Time: 15 minutes plus refrigerating   *Bake Time:* 1 hour plus standing

   1 cup butter-flavored cracker crumbs (about 40 crackers)
   ¼ cup (½ stick) butter *or* margarine, melted
   2 packages (8 ounces each) PHILADELPHIA® Cream Cheese, softened
   1 cup ricotta cheese
   3 eggs
   ½ cup KRAFT® 100% Grated Parmesan Cheese
   ½ cup DI GIORNO® Pesto
   ½ cup drained roasted red peppers, puréed

MIX crumbs and butter. Press onto bottom of 9-inch springform pan. Bake at 325°F for 10 minutes.

MIX cream cheese and ricotta cheese with electric mixer on medium speed until well blended. Add eggs, 1 at a time, mixing well after each addition. Blend in remaining ingredients. Pour over crust.

BAKE at 325°F for 55 minutes to 1 hour or until center is almost set. Run knife or metal spatula around rim of pan to loosen cake; cool before removing rim of pan. Refrigerate 4 hours or overnight. Let stand at room temperature 15 minutes before serving. Store leftover cheesecake in refrigerator.   ***Makes 12 to 14 servings***

Philadelphia® Cranberry Orange Spread

Prep Time: 5 minutes

   1 package (8 ounces) PHILADELPHIA® Cream Cheese, softened
   ½ cup cranberry orange sauce
   3 tablespoons chopped pecans, toasted

SPREAD cream cheese on serving plate.

TOP with sauce; sprinkle with pecans. Serve with crackers.   ***Makes 10 servings***

Creamy Feta & Sun-Dried Tomato Spread

Prep Time: 10 minutes plus refrigerating

1 package (8 ounces) PHILADELPHIA® Cream Cheese, softened
1 package (4 ounces) ATHENOS® Traditional Crumbled Feta Cheese
2 tablespoons chopped fresh basil
2 tablespoons finely chopped sun-dried tomatoes

MIX all ingredients. Refrigerate.

SERVE as a spread on NABISCO® Crackers or fresh vegetables.

Makes 1½ cups

Smoked Salmon Cheesecake

Prep Time: 15 minutes plus refrigerating   *Bake Time:* 1 hour

1 cup dry bread crumbs
3 tablespoons butter or margarine, melted
3 packages (8 ounces each) PHILADELPHIA® Cream Cheese, softened
4 eggs
½ pound smoked salmon, chopped
½ cup shredded KRAFT® Swiss Cheese
⅓ cup chopped green onions
2 to 3 tablespoons chopped fresh dill

MIX crumbs and butter. Press onto bottom of 9-inch springform pan. Bake at 325°F for 10 minutes.

MIX cream cheese and eggs with electric mixer on medium speed until well blended. Stir in remaining ingredients. Pour over crust.

BAKE at 325°F for 1 hour. Loosen cake from rim of pan; cool before removing from rim of pan. Refrigerate 4 hours or overnight.   *Makes 12 to 14 servings*

Spinach Cheese Triangles

Prep Time: 30 minutes   *Bake Time:* 15 minutes

> 1 package (8 ounces) PHILADELPHIA® Cream Cheese, softened
> 1 package (10 ounces) frozen chopped spinach, thawed, well drained
> 1/3 cup chopped drained roasted red peppers
> 1/4 teaspoon garlic salt
> 6 sheets frozen phyllo, thawed
> 1/2 cup (1 stick) butter or margarine, melted

MIX cream cheese, spinach, red peppers and garlic salt with electric mixer on medium speed until well blended.

LAY 1 phyllo sheet on flat surface. Brush with some of the melted butter. Cut lengthwise into 4 (18×3½-inch) strips.

SPOON about 1 tablespoon filling about 1 inch from one end of each strip. Fold the end over the filling at a 45-degree angle. Continue folding as you would fold a flag to form a triangle that encloses filling. Repeat procedure with remaining phyllo sheets. Place triangles on cookie sheet. Brush with melted butter.

BAKE at 375°F for 12 to 15 minutes or until golden brown.

Makes 3 dozen appetizers

Tip: Unfold phyllo sheets; cover with wax paper and damp towel to prevent drying until ready to use.

Philadelphia® Greek-Style Spread

Prep Time: 10 minutes

> 1 package (8 ounces) PHILADELPHIA® Cream Cheese, softened
> 1/2 cup chopped tomato
> 1/4 cup chopped pitted Niçoise olives
> 1/4 cup finely chopped cucumber
> 1 teaspoon olive oil
> 1/2 teaspoon dried oregano leaves, crushed

SPREAD cream cheese on serving plate.

MIX remaining ingredients; spoon over cream cheese. Serve with crackers or toasted pita wedges.

Makes 10 servings

Curried Chicken Puffs

$\frac{1}{2}$ cup water
$\frac{1}{3}$ cup butter or margarine
$\frac{2}{3}$ cup flour
   Dash of salt
 2 eggs
 1 package (8 ounces) PHILADELPHIA® Cream Cheese, softened
$\frac{1}{4}$ cup milk
$\frac{1}{4}$ teaspoon salt
   Dash of curry powder
   Dash of pepper
$1\frac{1}{2}$ cups chopped cooked chicken
$\frac{1}{3}$ cup slivered almonds, toasted
 2 tablespoons green onion slices

BRING water and butter to boil. Add flour and dash salt; stir vigorously over low heat until mixture forms ball. Remove from heat; add eggs, one at a time, beating until smooth after each addition.

PLACE level measuring tablespoonfuls of batter on ungreased cookie sheet.

BAKE at 400°F 25 minutes. Cool.

COMBINE cream cheese, milk, $\frac{1}{4}$ teaspoon salt, curry powder and pepper, mixing until well blended. Add chicken, almonds and onions; mix lightly.

CUT tops from cream puffs; fill with chicken mixture. Replace tops. Place puffs on cookie sheet.

BAKE at 375°F 5 minutes or until warm.

Makes approximately 1½ dozen appetizers

Note: Unfilled cream puffs can be prepared several weeks in advance and frozen. Place puffs on a jelly-roll pan and wrap securely in moisture-vaporproof wrap.

Three Pepper Quesadillas

Prep Time: 20 minutes   *Bake Time:* 10 minutes

 1 cup *each* **thin green, red and yellow pepper strips**
 ½ cup **thin onion slices**
 ½ teaspoon **ground cumin**
 ⅓ cup **butter** *or* **margarine**
 1 package (8 ounces) **PHILADELPHIA® Cream Cheese, softened**
 1 package (8 ounces) **KRAFT® Shredded Sharp Cheddar Cheese**
 10 **flour tortillas (6 inch)**
 TACO BELL® HOME ORIGINALS® Salsa

COOK and stir peppers, onion and cumin in butter in large skillet until tender-crisp, about 4 minutes. Drain, reserving butter.

MIX cream cheese and cheddar cheese until well blended. Spoon 2 tablespoons cheese mixture onto each tortilla; top with scant ⅓ cup pepper mixture. Fold tortillas in half; place on cookie sheet. Brush with reserved butter.

BAKE at 425°F for 10 minutes. Cut each tortilla into thirds. Serve warm with salsa.

Makes 30 appetizers

To Make Ahead: Prepare as directed except for baking; cover. Refrigerate. When ready to serve, bake, uncovered, at 425°F, 15 to 20 minutes or until thoroughly heated.

Philadelphia® Pesto Spread

Prep Time: 5 minutes

 1 package (8 ounces) **PHILADELPHIA® Cream Cheese, softened**
 ⅓ cup **DI GIORNO® Pesto Sauce**
 ⅓ cup **chopped tomatoes**

SPREAD cream cheese on serving plate.

TOP with pesto sauce; sprinkle with tomatoes. Serve with crackers.

Makes 10 servings

Divine Dips

Creamy Roasted Red Pepper Dip

Prep Time: 5 minutes plus refrigerating

1 package (8 ounces) PHILADELPHIA® Cream Cheese, softened
3 tablespoons milk
½ cup chopped, drained, roasted red peppers
½ teaspoon dried thyme leaves
⅛ teaspoon ground black pepper

MIX cream cheese and milk with electric mixer on medium speed until smooth. Blend in remaining ingredients. Refrigerate.

SERVE with NABISCO® Crackers or assorted cut-up vegetables.

Makes 1½ cups

Hot Artichoke Dip

Prep Time: 15 minutes   *Bake Time:* 25 minutes

1 package (8 ounces) PHILADELPHIA® Cream Cheese, softened
1 can (14 ounces) artichoke hearts, drained, chopped
½ cup KRAFT® Mayo Real Mayonnaise
½ cup KRAFT® 100% Grated Parmesan Cheese
1 clove garlic, minced

MIX all ingredients with electric mixer on medium speed until well blended. Spoon into 9-inch pie plate or quiche dish.

BAKE at 350°F for 20 to 25 minutes or until very lightly browned.

SERVE with NABISCO® Crackers, vegetable dippers or baked pita bread wedges.

Makes 2½ cups

Special Extras: To make baked pita bread wedges, cut each of 3 split pita breads into 8 triangles. Place on cookie sheet. Bake at 350°F for 10 to 12 minutes or until crisp.

Philadelphia® Fruit Dip

Prep Time: 5 minutes plus refrigerating

1 package (8 ounces) PHILADELPHIA® Cream Cheese, softened
1 container (8 ounces) strawberry *or* any flavored yogurt

MIX cream cheese and yogurt with electric mixer on medium speed until well blended. Refrigerate.

SERVE with assorted fresh fruit.

Makes about 1⅔ cups

Philadelphia® Cheddar Dip

Prep Time: 10 minutes plus refrigerating

- **1 package (8 ounces) PHILADELPHIA® Cream Cheese, softened**
- **3 tablespoons milk**
- **½ cup (2 ounces) KRAFT® Shredded Sharp Cheddar Cheese**
- **1 tablespoon chopped onion**
- **1 teaspoon Worcestershire sauce**

MIX cream cheese and milk with electric mixer on medium speed until smooth.

BLEND in remaining ingredients. Refrigerate. Serve with assorted cut-up vegetables, breadsticks or chips. *Makes 1⅓ cups*

Mediterranean Dip

Prep Time: 10 minutes plus refrigerating

- **1 package (8 ounces) PHILADELPHIA® Cream Cheese, softened**
- **2 tablespoons milk**
- **2 teaspoons red wine vinegar**
- **1 clove garlic, minced**
- **1 teaspoons lemon and pepper seasoning salt**
- **½ teaspoon dried oregano leaves, crushed**

MIX cream cheese, milk and vinegar with electric mixer on medium speed until smooth.

BLEND in remaining ingredients. Refrigerate. Serve with lavosh crackers or pita chips. *Makes 1 cup*

Cheesecake Cream Dip

Prep Time: 5 minutes plus refrigerating

1 package (8 ounces) PHILADELPHIA® Cream Cheese, softened
1 jar (7 ounces) marshmallow cream

MIX cream cheese and marshmallow cream until well blended. Refrigerate.

SERVE with assorted cut-up fruit, pound cake or cookies.　　*Makes 1½ cups*

Clam Appetizer Dip

Prep Time: 5 minutes plus refrigerating

1 can (6¼ ounces) minced clams
1 package (8 ounces) PHILADELPHIA® Cream Cheese, softened
2 teaspoons lemon juice
1½ teaspoons Worcestershire sauce
¼ teaspoon garlic salt
Dash of pepper

DRAIN clams, reserving ¼ cup liquid. Mix clams, reserved liquid and remaining ingredients until well blended. Refrigerate.

SERVE with potato chips or vegetable dippers.　　*Makes 1⅓ cups*

Spinach Dip

Prep Time: 10 minutes plus refrigerating

1 package (8 ounces) PHILADELPHIA® Cream Cheese, softened
¼ cup milk
1 package (10 ounces) frozen chopped spinach, thawed, drained
1 can (8 ounces) water chestnuts, drained, chopped
½ cup chopped red pepper
½ teaspoon garlic salt
⅛ teaspoon hot pepper sauce

MIX cream cheese and milk with electric mixer on medium speed until smooth. Blend in remaining ingredients. Refrigerate.

SERVE with assorted cut-up vegetables or potato chips.　　*Makes 3 cups*

Chili Cheese Dip

Prep Time: 5 minutes   *Microwave Time:* 3 minutes

1 package (8 ounces) PHILADELPHIA® Cream Cheese, softened
1 can (15 ounces) chili with *or* without beans
1 cup KRAFT® Shredded Cheddar Cheese

SPREAD cream cheese onto bottom and up sides of 9-inch microwavable pie plate or quiche dish. Spread chili over cream cheese. Sprinkle with cheddar cheese.

MICROWAVE on HIGH 3 minutes or until thoroughly heated.

SERVE hot with tortilla chips.   *Makes 3 cups*

Philadelphia® Bacon & Onion Dip

Prep Time: 10 minutes plus refrigerating

1 package (8 ounces) PHILADELPHIA® Cream Cheese, softened
3 tablespoons milk
6 slices OSCAR MAYER® Bacon, crisply cooked, crumbled
2 tablespoons sliced green onion
1 teaspoon KRAFT® Prepared Horseradish

MIX cream cheese and milk with electric mixer on medium speed until smooth.

BLEND in remaining ingredients. Refrigerate. Serve with assorted cut-up vegetables, breadsticks or chips.   *Makes 1½ cups*

7-Layer Mexican Dip

Prep Time: 10 minutes plus refrigerating

1 package (8 ounces) PHILADELPHIA® Cream Cheese, softened
1 tablespoon TACO BELL® HOME ORIGINALS® Taco Seasoning Mix
1 cup *each* guacamole, TACO BELL® HOME ORIGINALS® Thick 'N
    Chunky Salsa and shredded lettuce
1 cup KRAFT® Shredded Mild Cheddar Cheese
½ cup chopped green onions
2 tablespoons sliced pitted ripe olives

MIX cream cheese and seasoning mix. Spread onto bottom of 9-inch pie plate or quiche dish.

LAYER guacamole, salsa, lettuce, cheese, onions and olives over cream cheese mixture; cover. Refrigerate.

SERVE with NABISCO® Crackers or tortilla chips.   ***Makes 6 to 8 servings***

Great Substitutes: If your family doesn't like guacamole, try substituting 1 cup TACO BELL® HOME ORIGINALS® Refried Beans.

Philadelphia® Blue Cheese Dip

Prep Time: 5 minutes plus refrigerating

1 package (8 ounces) PHILADELPHIA® Cream Cheese, softened
3 tablespoons milk
½ cup KRAFT® Blue Cheese Crumbles
2 tablespoons chopped green onion

MIX cream cheese and milk with electric mixer on medium speed until smooth.

BLEND in remaining ingredients. Refrigerate. Serve with assorted cut-up vegetables or chips.   ***Makes 1⅓ cups***

Creamy Pesto Dip

Prep Time: 5 minutes plus refrigerating

1 package (8 ounces) PHILADELPHIA® Cream Cheese, softened
3 tablespoons milk
⅓ cup DI GIORNO® Basil Pesto Sauce
1 red pepper, finely chopped (about 1 cup)

MIX cream cheese and milk with electric mixer on medium speed until smooth. Blend in pesto and red pepper. Refrigerate.

SERVE with assorted NABISCO® Crackers, cut-up vegetables, breadsticks or chips.

Makes about 2⅓ cups

Philadelphia® Cajun Dip

Prep Time: 5 minutes plus refrigerating

1 package (8 ounces) PHILADELPHIA® Cream Cheese, softened
3 tablespoons milk
1 teaspoon ground red pepper
½ teaspoon garlic salt
½ teaspoon onion powder

MIX cream cheese and milk with electric mixer on medium speed until smooth.

BLEND in remaining ingredients. Refrigerate. Serve with assorted cut-up vegetables or chips.

Makes 1 cup

Creamy Salsa Dip

Prep Time: 10 minutes plus refrigerating

**1 package (8 ounces) PHILADELPHIA® Cream Cheese, softened
1 cup TACO BELL® HOME ORIGINALS® Salsa**

MIX cream cheese and salsa until well blended. Refrigerate.

SERVE with tortilla chips or assorted cut-up vegetables.   *Makes 2 cups*

Philadelphia® Dill Pickle Dip

Prep Time: 5 minutes plus refrigerating

**1 package (8 ounces) PHILADELPHIA® Cream Cheese, softened
3 tablespoons milk
1/2 cup chopped dill pickles**

MIX cream cheese and milk with electric mixer on medium speed until smooth.

BLEND in pickles. Refrigerate. Serve with assorted cut-up vegetables or chips.

Makes 1 1/2 cups

Caramel Apple Dip

Prep Time: 5 minutes

**1 package (8 ounces) PHILADELPHIA® Cream Cheese, softened
1/3 cup caramel ice cream topping
1/2 cup chopped peanuts
2 medium apples, cored, sliced**

SPREAD cream cheese on serving plate. Drizzle with topping; sprinkle with peanuts.

SERVE with apples.   *Makes 6 to 8 servings*

Tip: Dip can be made ahead and refrigerated overnight. Let stand at room temperature about 20 minutes before serving.

Roasted Red Pepper Dip

Prep Time: 15 minutes   *Chill Time:* 1 hour

> 1 (8-ounce) container **BREAKSTONE'S®** or **KNUDSEN®** Sour Cream
> 1 (7-ounce) jar roasted red peppers, drained
> 4 ounces **PHILADELPHIA®** Cream Cheese
> ½ teaspoon chopped fresh or frozen chives
>   Fresh chives, for garnish
>   **WHEAT THINS®** Snack Crackers

BLEND sour cream, peppers, cream cheese and chopped chives with electric mixer until well mixed.

SPOON into bowl; refrigerate for at least 1 hour.

GARNISH with chives if desired. Serve as dip with snack crackers.

Makes 2 cups

Hot Crab Dip

Prep Time: 10 minutes   *Bake Time:* 30 minutes

> 2 packages (8 ounces each) **PHILADELPHIA®** Cream Cheese, softened
> 2 cans (6 ounces each) crabmeat, rinsed, drained, flaked
> ½ cup **KRAFT®** Shredded Parmesan Cheese
> ¼ cup chopped green onions
> 2 teaspoons **KRAFT®** Prepared Horseradish

MIX all ingredients with electric mixer on medium speed until well blended. Spoon into 9-inch pie plate or quiche dish.

BAKE at 350°F for 25 to 30 minutes or until very lightly browned.

SERVE with crackers.

Makes 4 cups

Magic Dip

Prep Time: 5 minutes   *Microwave Time:* 4 minutes

1 package (8 ounces) PHILADELPHIA® Cream Cheese, softened
1 cup BAKER'S® Semi-Sweet Real Chocolate Chips
½ cup BAKER'S® ANGEL FLAKE® Coconut, toasted
½ cup chopped peanuts
 Graham crackers

SPREAD cream cheese onto bottom of 9-inch microwavable pie plate or quiche dish.

TOP with chocolate chips, coconut and peanuts.

MICROWAVE on MEDIUM (50% power) 3 to 4 minutes or until warm. Serve with graham crackers. Garnish, if desired.   *Makes 6 to 8 servings*

Philadelphia® Garlic & Herb Dip

Prep Time: 10 minutes plus refrigerating

1 package (8 ounces) PHILADELPHIA® Cream Cheese, softened
3 tablespoons milk
3 tablespoons finely chopped fresh basil
3 tablespoons finely chopped fresh parsley
2 tablespoons chopped fresh chives
1 clove garlic, minced

MIX cream cheese and milk with electric mixer on medium speed until smooth.

BLEND in remaining ingredients. Refrigerate. Serve with assorted cut-up vegetables, breadsticks or chips.   *Makes 1 cup*

Make-Your-Own Pepperoni "Pitzas"

Thick "Pitza" Sauce

- 1 (14½-oz) can diced tomatoes in juice
- 2 Tbsp olive oil
- 1 clove garlic, crushed through press
- ¼ tsp *each* dried oregano and sugar
- ⅛ tsp *each* salt and black pepper

"Pitza" Kit

- 2 Tbsp Thick "Pitza" Sauce
- 2 mini (4-in.) whole-wheat pita breads
- 2 heaping Tbsp shredded pizza-cheese blend
- 8 thin slices pepperoni (from 3.5-oz) pkg

1. THICK "PITZA" SAUCE: In small saucepan, uncovered, simmer together all ingredients 20 minutes, stirring several times, until most of liquid has cooked off. Let cool to room temperature, stirring occasionally to incorporate oil into sauce. When cool, mash with fork until sauce is thick but still slightly chunky. (You will have about 1 cup sauce, enough for 8 "Pitza" Kits; sauce can be refrigerated up to 2 weeks.)
2. "PITZA" KIT: Pack sauce in container with lid. Pack in insulated lunch box with ice pack, along with other Kit ingredients, each wrapped separately.
3. Spread 1 Tbsp sauce over each pita; top with cheese and pepperoni.

Makes 8 "Pitza" Kits. Per "Pitza" Kit with 2 Tbsp sauce: 383 calories, 15 g protein, 50 g carbohydrate, 15 g fat, 7 g fiber, 21 mg cholesterol, 959 mg sodium.

Green Beans With Creamy Parmesan Dip

Creamy Parmesan Dip

- ¼ cup +1 Tbsp light sour cream
- ¼ cup grated Parmesan cheese
- 2 Tbsp *each* olive oil and 82%-less-fat mayonnaise
- 1½ tsp cider vinegar
- 1 tsp soy sauce
- ¼ tsp sugar

Accompaniment

- 4 *each* green beans and yellow wax beans, cooked until crisp-tender, drained, cooled

1. CREAMY PARMESAN DIP: In mini food processor, blend all ingredients until thick and creamy. Makes about ⅔ cup dip, enough for 3 servings. (Can be refrigerated up to 2 days.)
2. Place 3 Tbsp Creamy Parmesan Dip into small plastic container with lid. Pack in insulated lunch box with beans and ice pack.

Makes 3 servings. Per serving with 3 Tbsp dip: 184 calories, 6 g protein, 9 g carbohydrate, 14 g fat, 1 g fiber, 15 mg cholesterol, 381 mg sodium.

Finger Lickin' Lunch Box

Oven-Fried Chicken Drumsticks *

Macaroni and Cheddar Cheese Salad *

Raspberry Applesauce Cup

Frozen Portable Yogurt Stick
* *Recipe follows*

Oven-Fried Chicken Drumsticks

- 8 chicken drumsticks (2½ lb)
- 1½ cups buttermilk
- 1 tsp garlic-flavored hot-red-pepper sauce
  Nonstick cooking spray
- 1 (4.2-oz) box extra-crispy coating mix for chicken
- ¼ cup grated Parmesan cheese

1. In 1-gallon resealable plastic food-storage bag, combine chicken, buttermilk and pepper sauce; seal bag. Refrigerate several hours or overnight.

2. Preheat oven to 400°F. Line rimmed baking sheet with aluminum foil. With cooking spray, coat foil. In bowl, stir together coating mix and cheese. Drain drumsticks; coat with coating mixture. Place on prepared baking sheet.
3. Bake 20 minutes; turn over. Bake 20 minutes or until crispy and chicken is cooked through. (Can be refrigerated up to 2 days.) Pack in insulated lunch box with ice pack.

Makes 8 drumsticks. Per drumstick: 223 calories, 22 g protein, 11 g carbohydrate, 10 g fat, 0 fiber, 62 mg cholesterol, 545 mg sodium.

Macaroni and Cheddar Cheese Salad

- ⅓ cup rotelle (wagon-wheel shape) pasta
- ½ oz yellow cheddar cheese, cut into small dice
- 2 Tbsp *each* finely diced, seeded plum tomato and celery
- 1½ Tbsp frozen green peas, thawed under running water, drained
- 1 Tbsp *each* 82%-less-fat mayonnaise and light sour cream
- 2 tsp *each* milk and sweet pickle relish
- ¼ tsp yellow mustard

1. Cook pasta following package directions; drain in colander. Rinse under cold water; drain.
2. In bowl, toss pasta with remaining ingredients until evenly coated. (Can be made 1 day ahead and refrigerated.) Pack in insulated lunch box with ice pack.

Makes ¾ cup, 1 serving. Per serving: 243 calories, 10 g protein, 34 g carbohydrate, 8 g fat, 2 g fiber, 21 mg cholesterol, 509 mg sodium. ▶

Good-for-them lunch-box fillers

Whole Kids, from the Whole Foods people, is America's first line of organic products especially for the younger set. The products are all natural and totally organic—and they're taste-tested by kids to please the pickiest eaters. Some of our favorite snacks: peanut butter, kid-size apples, string cheese, raisins and applesauce. For your nearest store, go to www.wholefoodsmarket.com.

2. With floured hands, form dough into flat round. Press evenly onto bottom and 1 in. up side of plate. Bake 25 to 30 minutes, until crust is lightly browned and puffy (soft in center). Let cool on rack (can be made several hours ahead).

3. To Assemble: In large bowl, mix peaches with remaining ½ cup granulated sugar. Let stand at room temperature, stirring occasionally, 30 minutes, until juicy. Spoon peaches with juice over crust, mounding peaches in center; scrape any juice clinging to bowl over peaches. In medium bowl, beat together cream and confectioners' sugar until stiff but billowy peaks form. Spoon over pie. Serve immediately, or refrigerate up to 6 hours.

Makes 8 servings. Per serving: 493 calories, 5 g protein, 56 g carbohydrate, 29 g fat, 3 g fiber, 91 mg cholesterol, 269 mg sodium.

For more information on Sara Foster, including the addresses of her two North Carolina restaurants, or to buy her products, go to the "Cooking" section of www.rosiemagazine.com.

233

Main & Side Dishes

Bacon and Creamy Fettuccine

Prep Time: 15 minutes   *Cook Time:* 25 minutes

1 package (16 ounces) OSCAR MAYER® Lower Sodium Bacon,
    cut into ½-inch pieces
8 ounces mushrooms, sliced
6 green onions, sliced
8 ounces fettuccine, uncooked
1 package (8 ounces) PHILADELPHIA FREE® Fat Free Cream
    Cheese, cubed
⅔ cup fat-free milk
½ teaspoon garlic powder
½ teaspoon dried basil leaves, crushed
½ teaspoon dried thyme leaves, crushed
1 small tomato, chopped

COOK bacon until crisp; drain. Add mushrooms and onions to bacon in skillet; cook and stir 4 minutes. Set aside.

MEANWHILE, cook fettuccine as directed on package in large saucepan; drain. Return fettuccine to saucepan; add cream cheese, milk and seasonings. Cook and stir on medium heat until cream cheese melts.

TOSS bacon mixture with fettuccine mixture; sprinkle with tomato.

Makes 6 servings

Cheesy Enchiladas

Prep Time: 15 minutes   *Bake Time:* 25 minutes

1 package (8 ounces) PHILADELPHIA FREE® Fat Free Cream Cheese, softened
1 package (8 ounces) KRAFT FREE® Fat Free Natural Shredded Non-Fat Cheddar Cheese, divided
¼ cup sliced green onions
6 flour tortillas (6 inch)
1 cup TACO BELL® HOME ORIGINALS® Thick 'N Chunky Salsa

BEAT cream cheese with electric mixer on medium speed until smooth. Add 1 cup of the cheddar cheese and onions, mixing until blended.

SPREAD ¼ cup cream cheese mixture down center of each tortilla; roll up. Place, seam-side down, in 11×7-inch baking dish. Pour salsa over tortillas. Sprinkle with remaining cheddar cheese; cover.

BAKE at 350°F for 20 to 25 minutes or until thoroughly heated.

Makes 6 servings

Sweet Potato Crisp

Prep Time: 20 minutes   *Bake Time:* 40 minutes

1 can (40 ounces) cut sweet potatoes, drained
1 package (8 ounces) PHILADELPHIA® Cream Cheese, softened
¾ cup firmly packed brown sugar, divided
¼ teaspoon ground cinnamon
1 cup chopped apples
⅔ cup chopped cranberries
½ cup flour
½ cup old-fashioned or quick-cooking oats, uncooked
⅓ cup butter or margarine
¼ cup chopped pecans

MIX sweet potatoes, cream cheese, ¼ cup of the sugar and cinnamon with electric mixer on medium speed until well blended. Spoon into 1½-quart casserole or 10×6-inch baking dish. Top with apples and cranberries.

MIX flour, oats and remaining ½ cup sugar in medium bowl; cut in butter until mixture resembles coarse crumbs. Stir in pecans. Sprinkle over fruit.

BAKE at 350°F for 35 to 40 minutes or until thoroughly heated.

Makes 8 servings

Chicken in Cream Sauce

Prep Time: 20 minutes   *Cook Time:* 20 minutes

4 boneless skinless chicken breast halves (about 1¼ pounds),
    cut into strips
1 medium red pepper, cut into strips
¼ cup sliced green onions
1 teaspoon Italian seasoning
½ teaspoon salt
2 tablespoons butter or margarine
¼ cup dry white wine, divided
1 package (8 ounces) PHILADELPHIA® Cream Cheese, cubed
½ cup milk
8 ounces linguine, cooked, drained

COOK chicken, vegetables and seasonings in butter in medium skillet on medium heat 10 minutes or until chicken is cooked through, stirring occasionally. Add 2 tablespoons wine; simmer 5 minutes.

STIR cream cheese, milk and remaining 2 tablespoons wine in small saucepan on low heat until smooth.

PLACE hot linguine on serving platter; top with chicken mixture and cream cheese mixture. Garnish, if desired.   *Makes 4 to 6 servings*

Creamy Rice with Bacon

Prep Time: 10 minutes   *Cook Time:* 30 minutes

1 clove garlic, minced
1 tablespoon butter or margarine
1 can (13¾ ounces) chicken broth
1 package (8 ounces) PHILADELPHIA® Cream Cheese, cubed
1 cup long grain rice, uncooked
½ cup frozen tiny peas, thawed, drained
2 slices OSCAR MAYER® Bacon, crisply cooked, crumbled

COOK and stir garlic in butter in medium saucepan until tender. Stir in broth. Bring to boil; reduce heat to low. Add cream cheese; stir until cream cheese is melted.

STIR in remaining ingredients; cover. Cook 20 minutes, stirring occasionally. Serve with Parmesan cheese, if desired.   *Makes 4 servings*

Layered Orange Pineapple Mold

Prep Time: 20 minutes   *Refrigerating Time:* 6 hours

> **1 can (20 ounces) crushed pineapple in juice, undrained**
> **Cold water**
> **1½ cups boiling water**
> **1 package (8-serving size) or 2 packages (4-serving size) JELL-O® Brand Orange Flavor Gelatin Dessert**
> **1 package (8 ounces) PHILADELPHIA® Cream Cheese, softened**

DRAIN pineapple, reserving juice. Add cold water to juice to make 1½ cups.

STIR boiling water into gelatin in large bowl at least 2 minutes until completely dissolved. Stir in measured pineapple juice and water. Reserve 1 cup gelatin at room temperature.

STIR ½ of the crushed pineapple into remaining gelatin. Pour into 6-cup mold. Refrigerate about 2 hours or until set but not firm (gelatin should stick to finger when touched and should mound).

STIR reserved 1 cup gelatin gradually into cream cheese in medium bowl with wire whisk until smooth. Stir in remaining crushed pineapple. Pour over gelatin layer in mold.

REFRIGERATE 4 hours or until firm. Unmold. Garnish as desired.

Makes 10 servings

Creamed Spinach Casserole

Prep Time: 10 minutes   *Bake Time:* 30 minutes

> **2 packages (10 ounces each) frozen chopped spinach, thawed, well drained**
> **2 packages (8 ounces each) PHILADELPHIA® Cream Cheese, softened**
> **1 teaspoon lemon and pepper seasoning salt**
> **⅓ cup crushed seasoned croutons**

MIX spinach, cream cheese and seasoning salt until well blended.

SPOON mixture into 1-quart casserole. Sprinkle with crushed croutons.

BAKE at 350°F for 25 to 30 minutes or until thoroughly heated.

Makes 6 to 8 servings

Grilled Turkey with Walnut Pesto Sauce

Prep Time: 15 minutes   *Cook Time:* 2 hours

1 (4- to 5½-pound) turkey breast
   Walnut Pesto Sauce (recipe follows)

PREPARE coals for grilling.

PLACE aluminum drip pan in center of charcoal grate under grilling rack. Arrange hot coals around drip pan.

PLACE turkey on greased grill. Grill, covered, 1½ to 2 hours or until internal temperature reaches 170°F.

SLICE turkey; serve with Walnut Pesto Sauce. Garnish with red and yellow pear-shaped cherry tomatoes, fresh chives and basil leaves, if desired.

Makes 12 servings

Walnut Pesto Sauce

1 container (8 ounces) PHILADELPHIA® LIGHT™ Light Soft Cream Cheese
1 (7-ounce) container refrigerated prepared pesto
½ cup finely chopped walnuts, toasted
⅓ cup milk
1 garlic clove, minced
⅛ teaspoon ground red pepper

STIR together all ingredients in small bowl until well blended. Serve chilled or at room temperature.

Chicken Ragout with Orzo

Prep Time: 30 minutes   *Cook Time:* 40 minutes

¾ cup (4 ounces) orzo, cooked and drained
1 tablespoon olive oil
⅔ cup chopped onion
1 can (4 ounces) mushrooms, drained
⅓ cup celery slices
⅓ cup finely chopped carrots
¼ pound Italian sausage, casing removed, crumbled
4 OSCAR MAYER® Bacon Slices, chopped
1½ pounds boneless, skinless chicken breasts, cut into ½-inch pieces
1 bay leaf
1 large clove garlic, minced
¾ cup dry Marsala wine
1 can (14½ ounces) tomatoes, cut up, undrained
1 cup chicken broth
⅛ teaspoon ground cloves
1 container (8 ounces) PHILADELPHIA FLAVORS® Sun Dried Tomato
  Cream Cheese

HEAT oil in Dutch oven over medium-high heat. Add onion, mushrooms, celery, carrots, sausage and bacon; cook and stir until vegetables are tender and sausage is browned, about 5 minutes.

ADD chicken, bay leaf and garlic; cook, stirring occasionally, 4 minutes.

ADD wine. Bring to a boil; reduce heat to low. Simmer 10 to 15 minutes or until only slight amount of liquid remains.

STIR in tomatoes, broth and cloves. Bring to a boil over medium-high heat; reduce heat to low. Simmer 20 minutes or until slightly thickened, stirring occasionally. Remove from heat.

STIR in cream cheese and orzo.   *Makes 6 servings*

Chicken Tetrazzini

Prep Time: 20 minutes   *Bake Time:* 30 minutes

½ **cup chopped onion**
½ **cup chopped celery**
¼ **cup (½ stick) butter or margarine**
1 **can (13¾ ounces) chicken broth**
1 **package (8 ounces) PHILADELPHIA® Cream Cheese, cubed**
¾ **cup (3 ounces) KRAFT® 100% Grated Parmesan Cheese, divided**
1 **package (7 ounces) spaghetti, cooked, drained**
1 **jar (6 ounces) whole mushrooms, drained**
1 **cup chopped cooked chicken or turkey**

COOK and stir onion and celery in butter in large skillet on medium heat until tender. Add broth, cream cheese and ½ cup Parmesan cheese; stir on low heat until cream cheese is melted.

ADD remaining ingredients except remaining Parmesan cheese; toss lightly. Spoon into 12×8-inch baking dish; sprinkle with remaining ¼ cup Parmesan cheese.

BAKE at 350°F for 30 minutes.   *Makes 6 servings*

Philadelphia® Mashed Potatoes

Prep Time: 10 minutes   *Cook Time:* 30 minutes

6 **cups (2 pounds) peeled quartered potatoes**
½ **cup milk**
1 **package (8 ounces) PHILADELPHIA® Cream Cheese, softened**
½ **teaspoon onion powder**
½ **to ¾ teaspoon salt**
¼ **teaspoon pepper**
   Paprika

PLACE potatoes and enough water to cover in 3-quart saucepan. Bring to boil. Reduce heat to medium; cook 20 to 25 minutes or until tender. Drain.

MASH potatoes, gradually stirring in milk, cream cheese, onion powder, salt and pepper until light and fluffy. Sprinkle with paprika. Serve immediately.

Makes 8 servings

To Make Ahead: Prepare as directed. Spoon into 1½-quart casserole; cover. Refrigerate overnight. When ready to serve, bake, uncovered, at 350°F for 1 hour or until thoroughly heated.

Chicken Tostadas

Prep Time: 20 minutes

> 3 cups shredded cooked chicken
> 1½ cups salsa
> 8 tostada shells
> 1 container (8 ounces) PHILADELPHIA® LIGHT™ Light Soft
>   Cream Cheese
> 1½ cups shredded lettuce
> 1 tomato, chopped
> 1 package (8 ounces) KRAFT® Shredded Mild Reduced Fat Cheddar
>   Cheese

TOSS chicken with salsa.

SPREAD tostada shells with cream cheese product; top with chicken mixture, lettuce, tomatoes and cheese. Serve with additional salsa and jalapeño pepper slices, if desired.

Makes 8 servings

Easy Fettuccine Alfredo

Prep Time: 15 minutes   *Cook Time:* 10 minutes

> 1 package (8 ounces) PHILADELPHIA® Cream Cheese, cubed
> 1 cup (4 ounces) KRAFT® Shredded Parmesan Cheese
> ½ cup (1 stick) butter or margarine
> ½ cup milk
> 8 ounces fettuccine, cooked, drained

STIR cream cheese, Parmesan cheese, butter and milk in large saucepan on low heat until smooth.

ADD fettuccine; toss lightly. Serve with additional Parmesan cheese, if desired.

Makes 4 servings

Chicken Tostada

Twice-Baked Potatoes

Prep Time: 10 minutes plus baking potatoes   *Bake Time:* 25 minutes

4 large baking potatoes, baked
1 package (8 ounces) PHILADELPHIA® Cream Cheese, softened
⅓ cup milk
½ teaspoon salt
Dash pepper
¼ cup chopped green onions
Paprika

CUT potatoes in half lengthwise; scoop out centers, leaving ⅛-inch shell.

MASH potatoes and cream cheese. Add milk and seasonings; beat until fluffy. Stir in onions; spoon into shells. Place on cookie sheet. Sprinkle with paprika.

BAKE at 350°F for 20 to 25 minutes or until thoroughly heated.

Makes 8 servings

Salmon Tortellini

Prep Time: 25 minutes

1 package (7 ounces) cheese-filled tortellini, cooked and drained
1 container (8 ounces) PHILADELPHIA® Soft Cream Cheese with Smoked Salmon
½ cup finely chopped cucumber
1 teaspoon dried dill weed *or* 2 teaspoons fresh dill

TOSS hot tortellini with remaining ingredients. Serve immediately.

Makes 6 to 8 servings

Layered Pear Cream Cheese Mold

Prep Time: 30 minutes   *Refrigerating Time:* 5 hours

    1 can (16 ounces) pear halves, undrained
    1 package (8-serving size) or 2 packages (4-serving size) JELL-O® Brand
        Lime Flavor Gelatin Dessert
1½ cups cold ginger ale or water
    2 tablespoons lemon juice
    1 package (8 ounces) PHILADELPHIA® Cream Cheese, softened
 ¼ cup chopped pecans

DRAIN pears, reserving liquid. Dice pears; set aside. Add water to liquid to make 1½ cups; bring to boil in small saucepan.

STIR boiling liquid into gelatin in large bowl at least 2 minutes until completely dissolved. Stir in cold ginger ale and lemon juice. Reserve 2½ cups gelatin at room temperature. Pour remaining gelatin into 5-cup mold. Refrigerate about 30 minutes or until thickened (spoon drawn through leaves definite impression). Arrange about ½ cup of the diced pears in thickened gelatin in mold.

STIR reserved 2½ cups gelatin gradually into cream cheese in large bowl with wire whisk until smooth. Refrigerate about 30 minutes or until slightly thickened (consistency of unbeaten egg whites). Stir in remaining diced pears and pecans. Spoon over gelatin layer in mold.

REFRIGERATE 4 hours or until firm. Unmold. Garnish as desired.

Makes 10 servings

Veggies in Cream Sauce

Prep Time: 10 minutes   *Microwave Time:* 13 minutes

    1 package (16 ounces) frozen broccoli, cauliflower and carrots
¼ pound (4 ounces) VELVEETA® Pasteurized Prepared Cheese Product,
    cut up
 4 ounces PHILADELPHIA® Cream Cheese, cubed

LAYER vegetables, Velveeta and cream cheese in 1½-quart microwavable casserole; cover.

MICROWAVE on HIGH 7 minutes; stir. Microwave 6 minutes or until vegetables are thoroughly heated.

STIR until creamy.

Makes 3 cups

Seafood Quiche

Prep Time: 15 minutes   *Bake Time:* 40 minutes plus standing

> 1 package (8 ounces) PHILADELPHIA® Cream Cheese, softened
> 1 can (6 ounces) crabmeat, drained, flaked
> 4 eggs
> ½ cup sliced green onions
> ½ cup milk
> ½ teaspoon dill weed
> ½ teaspoon lemon and pepper seasoning salt
> 1 (9-inch) baked pastry shell

MIX all ingredients except pastry shell with electric mixer on medium speed until well blended.

POUR into pastry shell.

BAKE at 350°F for 40 minutes or until knife inserted in center comes out clean. Let stand 10 minutes before serving.   ***Makes 6 to 8 servings***

Serving Suggestion: For a luncheon or light dinner, serve with fresh-cut melon slices.

Creamy Italian Chicken Fettuccine

Prep Time: 5 minutes   *Cook Time:* 15 minutes

> 8 ounces fettuccine, uncooked
> 3 cups cut-up assorted fresh vegetables
> 2 tablespoons olive oil
> ½ pound boneless skinless chicken breasts, cut into strips
> 1 cup milk
> ½ package (4 ounces) PHILADELPHIA® Cream Cheese, cubed
> 1 cup KRAFT® Shredded Parmesan Cheese, divided

PREPARE pasta as directed on package, adding vegetables during last 3 minutes of cooking time; drain.

HEAT oil in skillet on medium heat. Add chicken; cook and stir 8 minutes or until cooked through. Remove chicken; set aside.

HEAT milk, cream cheese and ¾ cup of the Parmesan cheese in skillet on low heat, stirring constantly until mixture is smooth. Toss all ingredients. Sprinkle with remaining ¼ cup Parmesan cheese.   ***Makes 4 servings***

Variation: Substitute 1½ cups chopped shrimp for cooked chicken.

Chicken Enchiladas

Prep Time: 20 minutes   *Bake Time:* 20 minutes

2 cups chopped cooked chicken or turkey
1 cup chopped green bell pepper
1 package (8 ounces) PHILADELPHIA® Cream Cheese, cubed
1 jar (8 ounces) salsa, divided
8 (6-inch) flour tortillas
¾ pound (12 ounces) VELVEETA® Pasteurized Process Cheese Spread,
    cut up
¼ cup milk

STIR chicken, bell pepper, cream cheese and ½ cup salsa in saucepan on low heat until cream cheese is melted.

SPOON ⅓ cup chicken mixture down center of each tortilla; roll up. Place, seam-side down, in lightly greased 12×8-inch baking dish.

STIR process cheese spread and milk in saucepan on low heat until smooth. Pour sauce over tortillas; cover with foil.

BAKE at 350°F for 20 minutes or until thoroughly heated. Pour remaining salsa over tortillas.   ***Makes 4 to 6 servings***

Creamy Tortellini

Prep Time: 20 minutes   *Cook Time:* 10 minutes

1 package (8 ounces) PHILADELPHIA® Cream Cheese, cubed
⅓ cup milk
½ cup chopped cucumber
3 ounces smoked salmon, cut into thin strips
2 teaspoon chopped fresh dill *or* ½ teaspoon dill weed
1 package (9 ounces) DI GIORNO® Cheese Tortellini, cooked, drained

STIR cream cheese and milk in medium saucepan on low heat until smooth. Add cucumber, salmon and dill; heat thoroughly.

TOSS with hot tortellini. Garnish with additional fresh dill.   ***Makes 4 servings***

Creamy Bow Tie Primavera

Prep Time: 15 minutes   *Cook Time:* 20 minutes

    8 ounces bow tie pasta, uncooked
    1 cup broccoli flowerets
    1 cup sliced carrots
    1 package (8 ounces) PHILADELPHIA FREE® Fat Free Cream Cheese,
        cubed
    ¾ cup fat-free milk
    ¼ cup KRAFT FREE® Nonfat Grated Topping
    ¼ cup chopped green onions
    ½ teaspoon Italian seasoning
    ¼ teaspoon garlic powder

PREPARE pasta as directed on package, adding broccoli and carrots to water during last 5 minutes of cooking time. Drain.

STIR cream cheese, milk, grated topping, onions and seasonings in large saucepan on low heat until cream cheese is melted.

ADD pasta and vegetables; toss lightly.   *Makes 6 servings*

Kid's Favorite Tuna Casserole

Prep Time: 15 minutes   *Cook Time:* 25 minutes

    ¾ pound VELVEETA® Pasteurized Prepared Cheese Product, cubed
    ⅔ cup milk
    1 package (3 ounces) PHILADELPHIA® Cream Cheese, cubed
    3 cups (6 ounces) medium noodles, cooked, drained
    1 package (10 ounces) frozen peas, thawed, drained
    1 can (6 ounces) tuna, drained, flaked
    1 cup crushed potato chips

PREHEAT oven to 350°F.

STIR together prepared cheese product, milk and cream cheese in saucepan over low heat until prepared cheese product is melted.

STIR in noodles, peas and tuna. Spoon into 2-quart casserole. Top with chips.

BAKE 20 to 25 minutes or until thoroughly heated.   *Makes 4 to 6 servings*

Eggplant Bulgur Casserole

Prep Time: 30 minutes   *Cook Time:* 25 minutes

   1 cup bulgur wheat
   ½ cup chopped green bell pepper
   ¼ cup chopped onion
   ¼ cup butter
   4 cups cubed peeled eggplant
   1 can (15 ounces) tomato sauce
   1 can (14½ ounces) tomatoes, undrained, cut up
   ½ cup cold water
   ½ teaspoon dried oregano leaves, crushed
   1 package (8 ounces) PHILADELPHIA® Cream Cheese, softened
   1 egg
      KRAFT® 100% Grated Parmesan Cheese

PREHEAT oven to 350°F.

SAUTÉ bulgur wheat, pepper and onion in butter in large skillet until vegetables are tender.

STIR in eggplant, tomato sauce, tomatoes, water and oregano. Cover; simmer 15 to 20 minutes or until eggplant is tender, stirring occasionally.

BEAT cream cheese and egg in small mixing bowl at medium speed with electric mixer until well blended.

PLACE half of vegetable mixture in 1½-quart baking dish or casserole; top with cream cheese mixture and remaining vegetable mixture. Cover.

BAKE 15 minutes. Remove cover; sprinkle with Parmesan cheese. Continue baking 10 minutes or until thoroughly heated.   ***Makes 8 to 10 servings***

Heavenly Cheesecakes

Philadelphia® 3-Step® Chocolate Lover's Cheesecake

Prep Time: 10 minutes   *Bake Time:* 40 minutes

2 packages (8 ounces each) PHILADELPHIA® Cream Cheese, softened
½ cup sugar
½ teaspoon vanilla
2 eggs
4 squares BAKER'S® Semi-Sweet Chocolate, melted, slightly cooled
1 ready-to-use chocolate flavor crumb crust (6 ounces or 9 inch)

MIX cream cheese, sugar and vanilla at medium speed with electric mixer until well blended. Add eggs; mix until blended. Stir in melted chocolate.

POUR into crust.

BAKE at 350°F for 35 to 40 minutes or until center is almost set. Cool. Garnish with fresh fruit. Refrigerate 3 hours or overnight.   ***Makes 8 servings***

Mocha: Blend 3 tablespoons coffee-flavored liqueur or black coffee into batter.

Philadelphia® 3-Step® Luscious Lemon Cheesecake

Prep Time: 10 minutes   *Bake Time:* 40 minutes

2 packages (8 ounces each) PHILADELPHIA® Cream Cheese, softened
½ **cup sugar**
1 tablespoon fresh lemon juice
½ **teaspoon grated lemon peel**
½ **teaspoon vanilla**
2 eggs
1 ready-to-use graham cracker crumb crust (6 ounces or 9 inch)

MIX cream cheese, sugar, juice, peel and vanilla with electric mixer on medium speed until well blended. Add eggs; mix until blended.

POUR into crust.

BAKE at 350°F for 40 minutes or until center is almost set. Cool. Refrigerate 3 hours or overnight. Garnish with COOL WHIP® Whipped Topping and lemon slices.

Makes 8 servings

Chocolate Chip Cheesecake

Prep Time: 10 minutes plus refrigerating   *Bake Time:* 40 minutes

2 packages (8 ounces each) PHILADELPHIA® Cream Cheese, softened
½ **cup sugar**
½ **teaspoon vanilla**
2 eggs
¾ **cup mini semi-sweet chocolate chips, divided**
1 ready-to-use graham cracker *or* chocolate flavor crumb crust (6 ounces or 9 inch)

MIX cream cheese, sugar and vanilla at medium speed with electric mixer until well blended. Add eggs; mix until blended. Stir in ½ cup of the chips.

POUR into crust. Sprinkle with remaining ¼ cup chips.

BAKE at 350°F for 40 minutes or until center is almost set. Cool. Refrigerate 3 hours or overnight.

Makes 8 servings

Peanut Butter Chocolate Chip Cheesecake: Beat in ⅓ cup peanut butter with cream cheese.

Banana Chocolate Chip Cheesecake: Beat in ½ cup mashed ripe banana with cream cheese.

Philadelphia® 3-Step® Luscious Lemon Cheesecake

Philadelphia® 3-Step® Midwest Cheesecake

Prep Time: 10 minutes   *Bake Time:* 40 minutes

- 2 packages (8 ounces each) **PHILADELPHIA**® Cream Cheese, softened
- ½ **cup sugar**
- ½ **teaspoon vanilla**
- 2 **eggs**
- 1 **ready-to-use graham cracker crumb crust (6 ounces or 9 inch)**
- ½ **cup sour cream**
- 3 **cups whole strawberries, stems removed**
- 2 **tablespoons strawberry jelly, heated**

MIX cream cheese, sugar and vanilla at medium speed with electric mixer until well blended. Add eggs; mix until blended.

POUR into crust.

BAKE at 350°F for 40 minutes or until center is almost set. Cool. Refrigerate 3 hours or overnight. Spread sour cream over cheesecake. Top with strawberries, stem-side down. Drizzle with jelly.   ***Makes 8 servings***

Philadelphia® 3-Step® Pralines and Cream Cheesecake

Prep Time: 10 minutes   *Bake Time:* 40 minutes

- 2 packages (8 ounces each) **PHILADELPHIA**® Cream Cheese, softened
- ½ **cup sugar**
- ½ **teaspoon vanilla**
- 2 **eggs**
- ½ **cup almond brickle chips**
- 1 **ready-to-use graham cracker crumb crust (6 ounces or 9 inch)**
- 3 **tablespoons caramel ice cream topping**

MIX cream cheese, sugar and vanilla at medium speed with electric mixer until well blended. Add eggs; mix until blended. Blend in almond brickle chips.

POUR into crust. Dot top of cheesecake batter with topping. Cut through batter with knife several times for marble effect.

BAKE at 350°F for 40 minutes or until center is almost set. Cool. Refrigerate 3 hours or overnight.   ***Makes 8 servings***

Philadelphia® 3-Step® Pumpkin Layer Cheesecake

Prep Time: 10 minutes plus refrigerating   *Bake Time:* 40 minutes

2 packages (8 ounces each) PHILADELPHIA® Cream Cheese, softened
½ cup sugar
½ teaspoon vanilla
2 eggs
½ cup canned pumpkin
½ teaspoon ground cinnamon
    Dash *each* ground cloves and nutmeg
1 ready-to-use graham cracker crumb crust (6 ounces or 9 inch)

MIX cream cheese, sugar and vanilla with electric mixer on medium speed until well blended. Add eggs; mix until blended.

STIR pumpkin and spices into 1 cup of the batter; pour remaining plain batter into crust. Top with pumpkin batter.

BAKE at 350°F for 35 to 40 minutes or until center is almost set. Cool. Refrigerate 3 hours or overnight. Store leftover cheesecake in refrigerator.   ***Makes 8 servings***

Fluffy 2-Step Chocolate Cheesecake

Prep Time: 10 minutes plus refrigerating

1 package (8 ounces) PHILADELPHIA® Cream Cheese, softened
⅓ cup sugar
1 package (4 ounces) BAKER'S® Semi-Sweet Baking Chocolate, melted
1 tub (8 ounces) COOL WHIP® Whipped Topping, thawed
1 ready-to-use graham cracker crumb crust (6 ounces or 9 inch)

MIX cream cheese, sugar and chocolate in large bowl with electric mixer on medium speed until well blended. Gently stir in whipped topping.

SPOON into crust. Refrigerate 3 hours or until set. Store leftover cheesecake in refrigerator.   ***Makes 8 servings***

Chocolate Raspberry Cheesecake

18 chocolate sandwich cookies, finely crushed
2 tablespoons butter or margarine, melted
3 packages (8 ounces each) PHILADELPHIA® Cream Cheese, softened
¾ cup sugar
1 teaspoon vanilla
3 eggs
½ cup BREAKSTONE'S® *or* KNUDSEN® Sour Cream
1 package (8 ounces) PHILADELPHIA® Cream Cheese, softened
6 squares BAKER'S® Semi-Sweet Chocolate, melted, slightly cooled
⅓ cup strained red raspberry preserves
6 squares BAKER'S® Semi-Sweet Baking Chocolate
¼ cup whipping cream

MIX crumbs and butter; press onto bottom of 9-inch springform pan.

BEAT 3 packages of the cream cheese, sugar and vanilla with electric mixer on medium speed with electric mixer until well blended. Add eggs, 1 at a time, mixing on low speed after each addition, just until blended. Blend in sour cream; pour over crust.

BEAT 1 package cream cheese and 6 squares melted chocolate with electric mixer on medium speed until well blended. Add preserves; mix well. Drop rounded tablespoonfuls of chocolate mixture over plain cream cheese mixture; do not swirl.

BAKE at 325°F for 1 hour and 15 minutes to 1 hour and 20 minutes or until center is almost set. Run knife or metal spatula around rim of pan to loosen cake; cool before removing rim of pan.

MELT remaining chocolate and whipping cream on low heat, stirring until smooth. Spread over cooled cheesecake. Refrigerate 4 hours or overnight. Garnish with additional whipped cream, raspberries and mint leaves. ***Makes 12 servings***

Citrus Fruit Cheesecake

Prep Time: 20 minutes plus refrigerating   *Bake Time:* 1 hour 5 minutes

Crust

    1 cup graham cracker crumbs
    ⅓ cup firmly packed brown sugar
    ¼ cup (½ stick) butter *or* margarine, melted

Filling

    4 packages (8 ounces each) PHILADELPHIA® Cream Cheese, softened
    1 cup granulated sugar
    2 tablespoons flour
    1 teaspoon vanilla
    1 tablespoons *each* fresh lemon juice, lime juice and orange juice
    ½ teaspoon *each* grated lemon peel, lime peel and orange peel
    4 eggs

Crust

MIX crumbs, brown sugar and butter; press onto bottom of 9-inch springform pan. Bake at 325°F for 10 minutes if using a silver springform pan. (Bake at 300°F for 10 minutes if using a dark nonstick springform pan.)

Filling

MIX cream cheese, granulated sugar, flour and vanilla with electric mixer on medium speed until well blended. Blend in juices and peel. Add eggs, mixing on low speed just until blended. Pour over crust.

BAKE at 325°F for 1 hour and 5 minutes or until center is almost set if using a silver springform pan. (Bake at 300°F for 1 hour and 5 minutes or until center is almost set if using a dark nonstick springform pan.) Run knife or metal spatula around rim of pan to loosen cake; cool before removing rim of pan. Refrigerate 4 hours or overnight.

Makes 12 servings

Café Latte Cheesecake

Prep Time: 25 minutes plus refrigerating   *Bake Time:* 1 hour 5 minutes

Crust
>   1 cup vanilla wafer cookie crumbs
>   3 tablespoons sugar
>   3 tablespoon butter *or* margarine, melted

Filling
>   4 packages (8 ounces each) PHILADELPHIA® Cream Cheese, softened
>   1 cup sugar
>   1 tablespoon vanilla
>   4 eggs
>   3 tablespoons MAXWELL HOUSE® Instant Coffee
>   1 tablespoon warm water
>   3 tablespoons milk

Crust

MIX crumbs, sugar and butter in small bowl; press onto bottom of 9-inch springform pan. Bake at 325°F for 10 minutes if using a silver springform pan. (Bake at 300°F for 10 minutes if using a dark nonstick springform pan.)

Filling

MIX cream cheese, sugar and vanilla with electric mixer on medium speed until well blended. Add eggs, mixing on low speed just until blended. Reserve 1½ cups of the batter. Stir instant coffee into warm water until dissolved. Add to remaining batter; mix well. Pour over crust. Stir milk into reserved batter; pour gently over coffee batter.

BAKE at 325°F for 1 hour 5 minutes or until center is almost set if using a silver springform pan. (Bake at 300°F for 1 hour 5 minutes or until center is almost set if using a dark nonstick springform pan.) Run knife or metal spatula around rim of pan to loosen cake; cool before removing rim of pan. Refrigerate 4 hours or overnight.

Makes 12 servings

Philadelphia® 3-Step® Cheesecake

Prep Time: 10 minutes   *Bake Time:* 40 minutes

**2 packages (8 ounces each) PHILADELPHIA® Cream Cheese *or*
PHILADELPHIA® Neufchâtel Cheese, ⅓ Less Fat than Cream
Cheese, softened**
½ cup sugar
½ teaspoon vanilla
2 eggs
1 ready-to-use graham cracker crumb crust (6 ounces or 9 inch)

MIX cream cheese, sugar and vanilla with electric mixer on medium speed until well
blended. Add eggs; mix until blended.

POUR into crust.

BAKE at 350°F for 40 minutes or until center is almost set. Cool. Refrigerate 3 hours
or overnight.   *Makes 8 servings*

Creamy 2-Step Pumpkin Cheesecake

Prep Time: 5 minutes plus refrigerating

1 package (8 ounces) PHILADELPHIA® Cream Cheese, softened
1 cup canned pumpkin
½ cup sugar
½ teaspoon pumpkin pie spice
1 tub (8 ounces) COOL WHIP® Whipped Topping, thawed
1 ready-to-use graham cracker crumb crust (6 ounces or 9 inch)

MIX cream cheese, pumpkin, sugar and pumpkin pie spice with electric mixer on
medium speed until smooth. Gently stir in whipped topping. Spoon into crust.

REFRIGERATE 3 hours or until set. Store leftover cheesecake in refrigerator.

Makes 8 servings

Double Lemon Cheesecake

Prep Time: 35 minutes plus refrigerating   *Bake Time:* 55 minutes

Crust
- 1 cup vanilla wafer cookie crumbs
- 3 tablespoons sugar
- 3 tablespoons butter *or* margarine, melted

Filling
- 3 packages (8 ounces each) PHILADELPHIA® Cream Cheese, softened
- 1 cup sugar
- 3 tablespoons flour
- 2 tablespoons lemon juice
- 1 tablespoon grated lemon peel
- ½ teaspoon vanilla
- 3 eggs
- 1 egg white

Topping
- ¾ cup sugar
- 2 tablespoons cornstarch
- ½ cup water
- ¼ cup lemon juice
- 1 egg yolk, beaten

Crust
MIX crumbs, sugar and butter; press onto bottom of 9-inch springform pan. Bake at 325°F for 10 minutes if using a silver springform pan.

Filling
MIX cream cheese, sugar, flour, juice, peel and vanilla with electric mixer on medium speed until well blended. Add 3 eggs and egg white, mixing on low speed just until blended. Pour over crust.

BAKE at 325°F for 50 to 55 minutes or until center is almost set if using a silver springform pan. Run knife or metal spatula around rim of pan to loosen cake; cool before removing rim of pan. Refrigerate 4 hours or overnight.

Topping
MIX sugar and cornstarch in saucepan; gradually stir in water and juice. Bring mixture to low boil on medium heat, stirring constantly until clear and thickened. Stir 2 tablespoons of the hot mixture into egg yolks; return to hot mixture. Cook 1 minute or until thickened, stirring constantly. Cool slightly. Spoon topping over cheesecake; refrigerate.

Makes 12 servings

Philadelphia® 3-Step® Creme Brûlée Cheesecake

Prep Time: 10 minutes   *Bake Time:* 40 minutes

2 packages (8 ounces each) PHILADELPHIA® Cream Cheese, softened
½ cup granulated sugar
1 teaspoon vanilla
2 eggs
1 egg yolk
1 ready-to-use graham cracker crumb crust (6 ounces or 9 inch)
½ cup packed brown sugar
1 teaspoon water

MIX cream cheese, granulated sugar and vanilla at medium speed with electric mixer until well blended. Add eggs and egg yolk; mix until blended.

POUR into crust.

BAKE at 350°F for 40 minutes or until center is almost set. Cool. Refrigerate 3 hours or overnight. Just before serving, heat broiler. Mix brown sugar and water; spread over cheesecake. Place on cookie sheet. Broil 4 to 6 inches from heat 1 to 1½ minutes or until topping is bubbly.   *Makes 8 servings*

Fruit Smoothie Cheesecake

Prep Time: 15 minutes plus freezing

2 packages (8 ounces each) PHILADELPHIA® Cream Cheese, softened
⅓ cup sugar
1 cup whole strawberries, puréed
1 ripe banana, puréed
1 tub (8 ounces) COOL WHIP® Whipped Topping, thawed
1 HONEY MAID® Honey Graham Pie Crust (9 inch)

MIX cream cheese and sugar with electric mixer on medium speed until well blended. Gently stir in puréed fruit and whipped topping. Spoon into crust.

FREEZE 4 hours or overnight until firm. Let stand at room temperature 1 hour or until cheesecake can be cut easily. Garnish with fresh strawberries.   *Makes 8 servings*

Helpful Hint: Soften the 2 packages (8 ounces each) cream cheese in microwave oven on HIGH 30 seconds or until softened.

Take a Shortcut: After puréeing fruits, add cream cheese and sugar to food processor to avoid using another bowl.

Philadelphia® 3-Step® Raspberry Swirl Cheesecake

Prep Time: 10 minutes   *Bake Time:* 40 minutes

> **2 packages (8 ounces each) PHILADELPHIA® Cream Cheese, softened**
> **½ cup sugar**
> **½ teaspoon vanilla**
> **2 eggs**
> **1 ready-to-use graham cracker crumb crust (6 ounces or 9 inch)**
> **3 tablespoons red raspberry preserves**

MIX cream cheese, sugar and vanilla at medium speed with electric mixer until well blended. Add eggs; mix until blended.

POUR into crust. Dot top of cheesecake with preserves. Cut through batter with knife several times for marble effect.

BAKE at 350°F for 40 minutes or until center is almost set. Cool. Refrigerate 3 hours or overnight. Garnish with COOL WHIP® Whipped Topping and raspberries.

Makes 8 servings

Peaches and Cream: Substitute ¼ cup peach preserves for red raspberry preserves.

Heavenly Orange Cheesecake

Prep Time: 25 minutes plus refrigerating

> **1 envelope unflavored gelatin**
> **½ cup orange juice**
> **3 packages (8 ounces each) PHILADELPHIA® Cream Cheese, softened**
> **¾ cup sugar**
> **1 tub (12 ounces) COOL WHIP® Whipped Topping, thawed**
> **1 tablespoon grated orange peel**
> **1 ready-to-use chocolate flavor crumb crust (6 ounces or 9 inch)**

SOFTEN gelatin in juice in small saucepan; stir over low heat until dissolved.

BEAT cream cheese and sugar on medium speed of electric mixer until well blended.

ADD gelatin mixture gradually, beating well after each addition. Refrigerate about 30 minutes or until slightly thickened.

GENTLY stir in whipped topping and peel; pour into crust. Refrigerate about 3 hours or until firm. Store leftover cheesecake in refrigerator. *Makes 8 servings*

Philadelphia® 3-Step® White Chocolate Almond Cheesecake

Prep Time: 10 minutes   *Bake Time:* 40 minutes

 2 packages (8 ounces each) PHILADELPHIA® Cream Cheese, softened
 ½ cup sugar
 ½ teaspoon vanilla
 2 eggs
 1 ready-to-use graham cracker crumb crust (6 ounces or 9 inch)
 1 package (6 squares) BAKER'S® Premium White Baking Chocolate, chopped, divided
 ½ cup chopped almonds

MIX cream cheese, sugar and vanilla with electric mixer on medium speed until well blended. Add eggs; mix until blended. Stir in ½ cup of the white chocolate.

POUR into crust. Sprinkle with almonds and remaining white chocolate.

BAKE at 350°F for 40 minutes or until center is almost set. Cool. Refrigerate 3 hours or overnight.   *Makes 8 servings*

Mini Cherry Cheesecakes

Prep Time: 15 minutes   *Freeze Time:* 3 hours

 12 NILLA® Wafers
 1 package (8 ounces) PHILADELPHIA® Cream Cheese, softened
 ¾ cup sugar
 1 tub (8 ounces) COOL WHIP® Whipped Topping, thawed
 1 cup cherry pie filling

PLACE 1 wafer into bottom of each of 12 (2½-inch) paper-lined muffin cups; set aside.

BEAT cream cheese and sugar with electric mixer on medium speed or wire whisk until light and fluffy. Stir in ½ of the whipped topping. Spoon filling into each cup, filling about ⅔ full. Top with cherry pie filling.

FREEZE 3 hours or until firm. To serve, let stand at room temperature 15 minutes. Serve with additional whipped topping, if desired.   *Makes 12 servings*

Helpful Hint: Soften cream cheese in microwave on HIGH 15 to 20 seconds.

Great Substitute: Strawberry, raspberry or lemon pie filling can be substituted for the cherry pie filling.

Eggnog Cheesecake

Prep Time: 25 minutes   *Bake Time:* 1 hour 15 minutes

Crust
    2 cups vanilla wafer crumbs
    6 tablespoons butter or margarine, melted
    ½ teaspoon ground nutmeg

Filling
    4 packages (8 ounces each) PHILADELPHIA® Cream Cheese, softened
    1 cup sugar
    3 tablespoons all-purpose flour
    3 tablespoons rum
    1 teaspoon vanilla
    2 eggs
    1 cup whipping cream
    4 egg yolks

HEAT oven to 325°F.

Crust
MIX crumbs, butter and nutmeg; press onto bottom and 1½-inches up sides of 9-inch springform pan. Bake 10 minutes.

Filling
BEAT cream cheese, sugar, flour, rum and vanilla at medium speed with electric mixer until well blended. Add eggs, 1 at a time, mixing at low speed after each addition, just until blended.

BLEND in cream and egg yolks; pour into crust.

BAKE 1 hour and 10 minutes to 1 hour and 15 minutes or until center is almost set. Run knife or metal spatula around rim of pan to loosen cake; cool before removing rim of pan. Refrigerate 4 hours or overnight. Garnish with COOL WHIP® Whipped Topping and ground nutmeg.   ***Makes 12 servings***

Autumn Cheesecake

Prep Time: 25 minutes plus refrigerating   *Bake Time:* 1 hour 15 minutes

Crust

1 cup graham cracker crumbs
½ cup finely chopped pecans
3 tablespoons sugar
½ teaspoon ground cinnamon
¼ cup (½ stick) butter *or* margarine, melted

Filling

2 packages (8 ounces each) PHILADELPHIA® Cream Cheese, softened
½ cup sugar
½ teaspoon vanilla
2 eggs

Topping

⅓ cup sugar
½ teaspoon ground cinnamon
4 cups thinly sliced peeled apples
¼ cup finely chopped pecans

Crust

MIX crumbs, pecans, sugar, cinnamon and butter; press onto bottom of 9-inch springform pan. Bake at 325°F for 10 minutes if using a silver springform pan. (Bake at 300°F for 10 minutes if using a dark nonstick springform pan.)

Filling

MIX cream cheese, sugar and vanilla with electric mixer on medium speed until well blended. Add eggs, mixing on low speed just until blended. Pour over crust.

Topping

MIX sugar and cinnamon; toss with apples. Spoon apple mixture over cream cheese layer; sprinkle with pecans.

BAKE at 325°F for 1 hour and 10 minutes to 1 hour and 15 minutes or until center is almost set if using a silver springform pan. (Bake at 300°F for 1 hour and 10 minutes to 1 hour and 15 minutes or until center is almost set if using a dark nonstick springform pan.) Run knife or metal spatula around rim of pan to loosen cake; cool before removing rim of pan. Refrigerate 4 hours or overnight.   ***Makes 12 servings***

Philadelphia® 3-Step® Fruit Topped Cheesecake

Prep Time: 10 minutes   *Bake Time:* 40 minutes

2 packages (8 ounces each) PHILADELPHIA® Cream Cheese, softened
½ cup sugar
½ teaspoon vanilla
2 eggs
1 ready-to-use graham cracker crumb crust (6 ounces or 9 inch)
2 cups sliced fresh fruit
2 tablespoons strawberry or apple jelly, heated (optional)

MIX cream cheese, sugar and vanilla with electric mixer on medium speed until well blended. Add eggs; mix until blended.

POUR into crust.

BAKE at 350°F for 40 minutes or until center is almost set. Cool. Refrigerate 3 hours or overnight. Top with fruit; drizzle with jelly, if desired.   *Makes 8 servings*

Philadelphia® 3-Step®
Crème de Menthe Cheesecake

Prep Time: 10 minutes   *Bake Time:* 40 minutes

2 packages (8 ounces each) PHILADELPHIA® Cream Cheese, softened
½ cup sugar
½ teaspoon vanilla
2 eggs
4 teaspoons green crème de menthe
1 ready-to-use chocolate flavor crumb crust (6 ounces or 9 inch)

MIX cream cheese, sugar and vanilla at medium speed with electric mixer until well blended. Add eggs; mix until blended. Blend in creme de menthe.

POUR into crust.

BAKE at 350°F for 40 minutes or until center is almost set. Cool. Refrigerate 3 hours or overnight. Garnish with chocolate leaves and twigs.   *Makes 8 servings*

Mint Bon Bon: Substitute ¼ teaspoon peppermint extract and a few drops green food coloring for crème de menthe. Stir ½ cup mini semi-sweet chocolate chips into batter. Sprinkle with additional ¼ cup chips before baking.

Philadelphia® 3-Step® Lime Cheesecake

Prep Time: 10 minutes   *Bake Time:* 40 minutes

2 packages (8 ounces each) PHILADELPHIA® Cream Cheese, softened
½ cup sugar
2 tablespoons fresh lime juice
1 teaspoon grated lime peel
½ teaspoon vanilla
2 eggs
1 ready-to-use graham cracker crumb crust (6 ounces or 9 inch)

MIX cream cheese, sugar, juice, peel and vanilla with electric mixer on medium speed until well blended. Add eggs; mix until blended.

POUR into crust.

BAKE at 350°F for 35 to 40 minutes or until center is almost set. Cool. Refrigerate 3 hours or overnight. Garnish with curled lemon peel.   ***Makes 8 servings***

Lemon Cheesecake: Prepare as directed, substituting 1 tablespoon fresh lemon juice for lime juice and ½ teaspoon grated lemon peel for lime peel.

Philadelphia® 3-Step® Rocky Road Cheesecake

Prep Time: 10 minutes   *Bake Time:* 40 minutes

2 packages (8 ounces each) PHILADELPHIA® Cream Cheese, softened
½ cup sugar
½ teaspoon vanilla
2 eggs
4 squares BAKER'S® Semi-Sweet Chocolate, melted, slightly cooled
1 ready-to-use graham cracker crumb crust (6 ounces or 9 inch)
½ cup miniature marshmallows
¼ cup BAKER'S® Semi-Sweet Real Chocolate Chips
¼ cup chopped peanuts

MIX cream cheese, sugar and vanilla at medium speed with electric mixer until well blended. Add eggs; mix until blended. Blend in melted chocolate.

POUR into crust. Sprinkle with marshmallows, chips and peanuts.

BAKE at 350°F for 40 minutes or until center is almost set. Cool. Refrigerate 3 hours or overnight. Garnish with multicolored sprinkles.   ***Makes 8 servings***

Philadelphia® 3-Step® Tirami Su Cheesecake

Prep Time: 10 minutes   *Bake Time:* 40 minutes

   2 packages (8 ounces each) PHILADELPHIA® Cream Cheese, softened
   ½ cup sugar
   ½ teaspoon vanilla
   2 eggs
   2 tablespoons brandy
  12 ladyfingers, split
   ½ cup strong black coffee
   1 cup COOL WHIP® Whipped Topping, thawed
   1 square BAKER'S® Semi-Sweet Chocolate, shaved

MIX cream cheese, sugar and vanilla with electric mixer on medium speed until well blended. Add eggs; mix until blended. Stir in brandy. Arrange ladyfingers on bottom and sides of 9-inch pie plate; drizzle with coffee.

POUR cream cheese mixture into prepared pie plate.

BAKE at 350°F for 40 minutes or until center is almost set. Cool. Refrigerate 3 hours or overnight. Top with whipped topping and shaved chocolate just before serving.

Makes 8 servings

Philadelphia® 3-Step® Toffee Crunch Cheesecake

Prep Time: 10 minutes   *Bake Time:* 40 minutes

   2 packages (8 ounces each) PHILADELPHIA® Cream Cheese, softened
   ½ cup firmly packed brown sugar
   ½ teaspoon vanilla
   2 eggs
   4 packages (1.4 ounces each) chocolate-covered English toffee bars,
       chopped (1 cup), divided
   1 ready-to-use graham cracker crumb crust (6 ounces or 9 inch)

MIX cream cheese, sugar and vanilla with electric mixer on medium speed until well blended. Add eggs; mix until blended. Stir in ¾ cup of the chopped toffee bars.

POUR into crust. Sprinkle with remaining toffee bars.

BAKE at 350°F for 35 to 40 minutes or until center is almost set. Cool. Refrigerate 3 hours or overnight.

Makes 8 servings

Brownie Bottom Cheesecake

Prep Time: 20 minutes plus refrigerating   *Bake Time:* 1 hour 5 minutes

   1 package (10 to 20 ounces) brownie mix, any variety
   3 packages (8 ounces each) PHILADELPHIA® Cream Cheese, softened
 ¾ cup sugar
   1 teaspoon vanilla
 ½ cup BREAKSTONE'S® *or* KNUDSEN® Sour Cream
   3 eggs

PREPARE and bake brownie mix as directed on package for 9-inch square pan in bottom of well-greased 9-inch springform pan.

MIX cream cheese, sugar and vanilla with electric mixer on medium speed until well blended. Blend in sour cream. Add eggs, mixing on low speed just until blended. Pour over brownie crust.

BAKE at 325°F for 1 hour to 1 hour and 5 minutes or until center is almost set if using a silver springform pan. (Bake at 300°F for 1 hour to 1 hour and 5 minutes or until center is almost set if using a dark nonstick springform pan.) Run knife or metal spatula around rim of pan to loosen cake; cool before removing rim of pan. Refrigerate 4 hours or overnight.

Makes 12 servings

Philadelphia® 3-Step® Blueberry Cheesecake

Prep Time: 10 minutes   *Bake Time:* 40 minutes

   2 packages (8 ounces each) PHILADELPHIA® Cream Cheese, softened
 ½ cup sugar
 ½ teaspoon vanilla
   2 eggs
   1 cup blueberries, divided
   1 ready-to-use graham cracker crumb crust (6 ounces or 9 inch)

MIX cream cheese, sugar and vanilla at medium speed with electric mixer until well blended. Add eggs; mix until blended. Stir in ½ cup of the blueberries.

POUR into crust. Sprinkle with remaining ½ cup blueberries.

BAKE at 350°F for 40 minutes or until center is almost set. Cool. Refrigerate 3 hours or overnight. Garnish with COOL WHIP® Whipped Topping and blueberries.

Makes 8 servings

Philadelphia® 3-Step® White Chocolate Raspberry Swirl Cheesecake

Prep Time: 10 minutes plus refrigerating   *Bake Time:* 40 minutes

2 packages (8 ounces each) PHILADELPHIA® Cream Cheese, softened
½ cup sugar
½ teaspoon vanilla
2 eggs
3 squares (3 ounces) BAKER'S® Premium White Baking Chocolate, melted
1 ready-to-use chocolate flavor crumb crust (6 ounces or 9 inch)
3 tablespoons red raspberry preserves

MIX cream cheese, sugar and vanilla with electric mixer on medium speed until well blended. Add eggs; mix until blended. Stir in white chocolate.

POUR into crust. Microwave preserves in small bowl on HIGH 15 seconds or until melted. Dot top of cheesecake with small spoonfuls of preserves. Cut through batter with knife several times for swirl effect.

BAKE at 350°F for 35 to 40 minutes or until center is almost set. Cool. Refrigerate 3 hours or overnight.   *Makes 8 servings*

Philadelphia® 3-Step® Caramel Apple Cheesecake

Prep Time: 10 minutes   *Bake Time:* 40 minutes

2 packages (8 ounces each) PHILADELPHIA® Cream Cheese, softened
½ cup sugar
½ teaspoon vanilla
2 eggs
⅓ cup frozen apple juice concentrate, thawed
1 ready-to-use graham cracker crumb crust (6 ounces or 9 inch)
¼ cup caramel ice cream topping
¼ cup chopped peanuts

MIX cream cheese, sugar and vanilla at medium speed with electric mixer until well blended. Add eggs; mix until blended. Blend in juice concentrate.

POUR into crust.

BAKE at 350°F for 40 minutes or until center is almost set. Cool. Refrigerate 3 hours or overnight. Drizzle with topping and sprinkle with peanuts before serving. Garnish with apple slices.   *Makes 8 servings*

Philadelphia® 3-Step® Mini Cheesecakes

Prep Time: 10 minutes   *Bake Time:* 20 minutes

2 packages (8 ounces each) PHILADELPHIA® Cream Cheese, softened
½ cup sugar
½ teaspoon vanilla
2 eggs
2 packages (4 ounces each) ready-to-use single serve graham cracker crusts (12 crusts)

MIX cream cheese, sugar and vanilla with electric mixer on medium speed until well blended. Add eggs; mix until blended.

POUR into crusts placed on cookie sheets

BAKE at 350°F for 20 minutes or until centers are almost set. Cool. Refrigerate 3 hours or overnight. Garnish with fresh fruit.   *Makes 12 servings*

Cappuccino Cheesecake

Prep Time: 25 minutes plus refrigerating   *Bake Time:* 1 hour

2 packages (8 ounces each) PHILADELPHIA® Cream Cheese, softened
½ cup sugar
1 envelope MAXWELL HOUSE® Cappucino, any flavor
2 eggs
¼ cup milk
1 ready-to-use graham cracker crumb crust (6 ounces or 9 inch)

MIX cream cheese, sugar and cappuccino in large bowl with electric mixer on medium speed until well blended. Add eggs and milk; mix until well blended. Pour into crust.

BAKE at 325°F for 40 minutes or until center is almost set. Cool.

REFRIGERATE 3 hours or overnight.   *Makes 12 servings*

Helpful Hint: Soften cream cheese in microwave on HIGH 15 to 20 seconds.

Chocolate Truffle Cheesecake

Prep Time: 30 minutes plus refrigerating   *Bake Time:* 1 hour

Crust
- 1½ **cups crushed chocolate sandwich cookies (about 18 cookies)**
- 2 **tablespoons butter** *or* **margarine, melted**

Filling
- 3 **packages (8 ounces each) PHILADELPHIA® Cream Cheese, softened**
- 1 **cup sugar**
- 1 **teaspoon vanilla**
- 8 **squares BAKER'S® Semi-Sweet Baking Chocolate, melted, slightly cooled**
- ¼ **cup hazelnut liqueur (optional)**
- 3 **eggs**

Crust

MIX crumbs and butter; press onto bottom of 9-inch springform pan. Bake at 325°F for 10 minutes if using a silver springform pan. (Bake at 300°F for 10 minutes if using a dark nonstick springform pan.)

Filling

MIX cream cheese, sugar and vanilla with electric mixer on medium speed until well blended. Blend in melted chocolate and liqueur. Add eggs, mixing on low speed just until blended. Pour over crust.

BAKE at 325°F for 55 to 60 minutes or until center is almost set if using a silver springform pan. (Bake at 300°F for 55 to 60 minutes or until center is almost set if using a dark nonstick springform pan.) Run knife or metal spatula around rim of pan to loosen cake; cool before removing rim of pan. Refrigerate 4 hours or overnight.

Makes 12 servings

Heavenly Cheesecake

Prep Time: 15 minutes   *Bake Time:* 50 minutes

  ½ **cup graham cracker crumbs**
  4 **packages (8 ounces each) PHILADELPHIA® Neufchâtel Cheese,**
      ⅓ **Less Fat than Cream Cheese**
  1 **cup sugar**
  ¼ **teaspoon almond extract** *or* 1 **teaspoon vanilla**
  2 **eggs**
  3 **egg whites**

HEAT oven to 325°F.

GREASE bottom of 9-inch springform pan. Sprinkle with crumbs.

BEAT Neufchâtel cheese, sugar and extract at medium speed with electric mixer until well blended. Add eggs and egg whites, 1 at a time, mixing at low speed after each addition, just until blended. Pour into pan.

BAKE 45 to 50 minutes or until center is almost set. Run knife or metal spatula around rim of pan to loosen cake; cool before removing rim of pan. Refrigerate 4 hours or overnight.

GARNISH with raspberries, strawberries or blueberries and mint leaves.

Makes 12 servings

Philadelphia® 3-Step® Cranberry Cheesecake

Prep Time: 10 minutes   *Bake Time:* 40 minutes

  2 **packages (8 ounces each) PHILADELPHIA® Cream Cheese, softened**
  ½ **cup sugar**
  ½ **teaspoon grated orange peel**
  ½ **teaspoon vanilla**
  2 **eggs**
  ¾ **cup chopped cranberries, divided**
  1 **ready-to-use graham cracker crumb crust (6 ounces or 9 inch)**

MIX cream cheese, sugar, peel and vanilla with electric mixer on medium speed until well blended. Add eggs; mix until blended. Stir in ½ cup of the cranberries.

POUR into crust. Sprinkle with remaining ¼ cup cranberries.

BAKE at 350°F for 40 minutes or until center is almost set. Cool. Refrigerate 3 hours or overnight. Garnish with additional cranberries, mint leaves and orange peel.

Makes 8 servings

Philadelphia® 3-Step® Chocolate Swirl Cheesecake

Prep Time: 10 minutes   *Bake Time:* 40 minutes

> **2 packages (8 ounces each) PHILADELPHIA® Cream Cheese, softened**
> **½ cup sugar**
> **½ teaspoon vanilla**
> **2 eggs**
> **1 square BAKER'S® Semi-Sweet Chocolate, melted, slightly cooled**
> **1 ready-to-use chocolate flavor crumb crust (6 ounces or 9 inch)**

MIX cream cheese, sugar and vanilla with electric mixer on medium speed until well blended. Add eggs; mix until blended. Stir melted chocolate into ¾ cup of the cream cheese batter.

POUR remaining cream cheese batter into crust. Spoon chocolate batter over cream cheese batter; cut through batter with knife several times for marble effect.

BAKE at 350°F for 35 to 40 minutes or until center is almost set. Cool. Refrigerate 3 hours or overnight.   *Makes 8 servings*

Philadelphia® 3-Step® Coconut Cheesecake

Prep Time: 10 minutes   *Bake Time:* 40 minutes

> **2 packages (8 ounces each) PHILADELPHIA® Cream Cheese, softened**
> **½ cup cream of coconut**
> **½ cup sugar**
> **½ teaspoon vanilla**
> **2 eggs**
> **1 ready-to-use graham cracker crumb crust (6 ounces or 9 inch)**
> **1 cup COOL WHIP® Whipped Topping, thawed**
> **½ cup BAKER'S® ANGEL FLAKE® Coconut, toasted**

MIX cream cheese, cream of coconut, sugar and vanilla at medium speed with electric mixer until well blended. Add eggs; mix until blended.

POUR into crust.

BAKE at 350°F for 40 minutes or until center is almost set. Cool. Refrigerate 3 hours or overnight. Top with whipped topping and toasted coconut before serving.
Makes 8 servings

Dazzling Desserts

Café Ladyfinger Dessert

Prep Time: 20 minutes   *Refrigerating Time:* 1 hour

2 packages (3 ounces each) ladyfingers, split, separated
1 cup freshly brewed strong MAXWELL HOUSE® or YUBAN®
    Coffee, any variety, at room temperature, divided
1 package (8 ounces) PHILADELPHIA FREE® Fat Free Cream
    Cheese
2 cups cold fat free milk
2 packages (4-serving size each) JELL-O® Vanilla Flavor Fat Free
    Sugar Free Instant Reduced Calorie Pudding & Pie Filling
1 tub (8 ounces) COOL WHIP FREE® Whipped Topping, thawed,
    divided

BRUSH cut side of ladyfingers with about ¼ cup of the coffee. Place ladyfingers on bottom and up side of 2-quart serving bowl.

BEAT cream cheese and remaining ¾ cup coffee in large bowl with wire whisk until smooth. Gradually beat in milk until smooth. Add pudding mixes. Beat with wire whisk 1 minute or until well blended. Gently stir in ½ of the whipped topping. Spoon into prepared bowl; cover.

REFRIGERATE 1 hour or until ready to serve. Top with remaining whipped topping.   *Makes 12 servings*

Special Extra: Garnish with 3 tablespoons shaved or chopped chocolate.

Berried Delight

Prep Time: 30 minutes   *Refrigerating Time:* 4 hours

  1½ cups graham cracker crumbs
   ½ cup sugar, divided
   ½ cup (1 stick) butter or margarine, melted
   1 package (8 ounces) PHILADELPHIA® Cream Cheese, softened
   2 tablespoons milk
   1 tub (8 ounces) COOL WHIP® Whipped Topping, thawed
   2 pints strawberries, hulled, halved
  3½ cups cold milk
   2 packages (4-serving size) JELL-O® Vanilla Flavor Instant Pudding
     & Pie Filling

MIX crumbs, ¼ cup of the sugar and butter in 13×9-inch pan. Press firmly onto bottom of pan. Refrigerate until ready to fill.

BEAT cream cheese, remaining ¼ cup sugar and 2 tablespoons milk until smooth. Gently stir in ½ of the whipped topping. Spread over crust. Top with strawberry halves.

POUR 3½ cups milk into large bowl. Add pudding mixes. Beat with wire whisk 2 minutes. Pour over cream cheese layer.

REFRIGERATE 4 hours or until set. Just before serving, spread remaining whipped topping over pudding.

Makes 15 servings

Crazy Colored Halloween Desserts

   1 package (8 ounces) PHILADELPHIA® Cream Cheese, softened
   4 scoops KOOL-AID® Sugar-Sweetened Soft Drink Mix, any green
     or orange flavor
  ½ cup milk
   1 tub (8 ounces) COOL WHIP® Whipped Topping, thawed
  12 sponge cake dessert shells
   Assorted candies and cookies

BEAT cream cheese and soft drink mix in large bowl until well blended. Gradually beat in milk until smooth. Gently stir in whipped topping.

SPOON about ⅓ cup whipped topping mixture into each dessert shell. Decorate with candies and cookies to resemble pumpkins, spiders and witches. Refrigerate until ready to serve.

Makes 12 servings

Napoleons

Prep Time: 20 minutes plus chilling   *Bake Time:* 10 minutes

1 frozen ready-to-bake puff pastry sheet
1 container (8 ounces) PHILADELPHIA® Soft Cream Cheese
¼ cup powdered sugar
¼ teaspoon almond extract
1 cup whipping cream, whipped
½ cup powdered sugar
1 tablespoon milk
1 (1 ounce) square BAKER'S® Semi-Sweet Baking Chocolate, melted

THAW puff pastry sheet according to package directions.

PREHEAT oven to 400°F.

ROLL pastry to 15×12-inch rectangle on lightly floured surface. Cut lengthwise into thirds.

PLACE pastry strips on large ungreased cookie sheet; prick pastry generously with fork. Bake 8 to 10 minutes or until light golden brown.

STIR together cream cheese, ¼ cup sugar and extract in medium bowl until well blended. Fold in whipped cream.

SPREAD two pastry strips with cream cheese mixture; stack. Top with remaining pastry strip.

STIR together ½ cup sugar and milk in small bowl until smooth. Spread over top pastry strip. Drizzle with melted chocolate. Chill.   ***Makes 10 servings***

Microwave Tip: Microwave chocolate in small bowl on HIGH 30 seconds to 1 minute or until chocolate begins to melt, stirring every 30 seconds. Stir until chocolate is completely melted.

Peanut Butter-Banana Brownie Pizza

Prep Time: 15 minutes   *Bake Time:* 20 minutes

    1 package (21½ ounces) brownie mix
    1 package (8 ounces) PHILADELPHIA® Cream Cheese, softened
    ¼ cup sugar
    ¼ cup creamy peanut butter
    3 large bananas, peeled, sliced
    ¼ cup coarsely chopped peanuts
    2 squares BAKER'S® Semi-Sweet Chocolate
    2 teaspoons butter or margarine

PREPARE brownie mix as directed on package. Spread batter evenly in greased 12-inch pizza pan. Bake 20 minutes. Cool completely on wire rack.

MIX cream cheese, sugar and peanut butter with electric mixer on medium speed until well blended. Spread over brownie. Arrange banana slices over cream cheese mixture; sprinkle with peanuts.

COOK chocolate and butter in heavy saucepan on very low heat, stirring constantly until just melted. Drizzle over bananas and peanuts.   ***Makes 12 servings***

Lemon Cheese Squares

    15 whole graham crackers, broken in half
    2 packages (8 ounces each) PHILADELPHIA® Cream Cheese, softened
    3 cups cold milk
    2 packages (6-serving size) JELL-O® Lemon Flavor Instant Pudding
       & Pie Filling
    1 tub (8 ounces) COOL WHIP® Whipped Topping, thawed
    1 can (21 ounces) blueberry pie filling

ARRANGE ½ of the crackers in bottom of 13×9-inch pan, cutting crackers to fit, if necessary.

BEAT cream cheese in large bowl with electric mixer on low speed until smooth. Gradually beat in 1 cup of the milk. Add remaining milk and pudding mixes. Beat 1 to 2 minutes. Gently stir in 2 cups of the whipped topping.

SPREAD ½ of the pudding mixture over crackers. Add second layer of crackers; top with remaining pudding mixture and whipped topping.

FREEZE 2 hours or until firm. Let stand at room temperature 15 minutes or until squares can be cut easily. Garnish with pie filling. Store leftover dessert in freezer.

Makes 18 servings

Holiday Cheesecake Presents

Prep Time: 10 minutes plus refrigerating   *Bake Time:* 30 minutes

  1½ **cups graham cracker crumbs**
   ⅓ **cup butter *or* margarine, melted**
   3 **tablespoons sugar**
   3 **packages (8 ounces each) PHILADELPHIA® Cream Cheese, softened**
   ¾ **cup sugar**
   1 **teaspoon vanilla**
   3 **eggs**

MIX crumbs, butter and 3 tablespoons sugar; press onto bottom of 13×9-inch baking pan.

MIX cream cheese, ¾ cup sugar and vanilla with electric mixer on medium speed until well blended. Add eggs; mix until blended. Pour over crust.

BAKE at 350°F for 30 minutes or until center is almost set. Cool. Refrigerate 3 hours or overnight. Cut into bars. Decorate bars with decorating gels and sprinkles to resemble presents. Store leftover bars in refrigerator.   ***Makes 2 dozen bars***

Black Forest Parfaits

Prep Time: 10 minutes

   1 **package (8 ounces) PHILADELPHIA® Cream Cheese, softened**
   2 **cups cold milk**
   1 **package (4-serving size) JELL-O® Chocolate Flavor Instant Pudding & Pie Filling**
   1 **can (21 ounces) cherry pie filling**
   1 **tablespoon cherry liqueur**
   ½ **cup chocolate wafer cookie crumbs**

BEAT cream cheese with ½ cup of the milk at low speed until smooth. Add pudding mix and remaining milk. Beat until smooth, 1 to 2 minutes.

MIX cherry pie filling and liqueur. Reserve a few cherries for garnish, if desired. Spoon ½ of pudding mixture evenly into individual dessert dishes; sprinkle with cookie crumbs. Top with pie filling, then with remaining pudding mixture. Refrigerate until ready to serve. Garnish with reserved cherries and additional cookie crumbs, if desired.   ***Makes 4 to 6 servings***

Tiramisu

Prep Time: 15 minutes plus refrigerating

⅓ cup **GENERAL FOODS INTERNATIONAL COFFEES®, Sugar Free Fat Free Suisse Mocha Flavor, divided**
2 **tablespoons hot water**
1 **package (3 ounces) ladyfingers, split**
2½ **cups cold fat-free milk, divided**
1 **container (8 ounces) PHILADELPHIA FREE® Soft Fat Free Cream Cheese**
2 **packages (4-serving size each) JELL-O® Vanilla Flavor Fat Free Sugar Free Instant Reduced Calorie Pudding & Pie Filling**
1 **cup COOL WHIP LITE® Whipped Topping, thawed**

DISSOLVE 1 tablespoon of the flavored instant coffee in hot water in small bowl.

COVER bottom and sides of shallow 2-quart dessert dish with ladyfingers. Sprinkle dissolved flavored instant coffee over ladyfingers.

PLACE ½ cup of the milk, cream cheese and remaining undissolved flavored instant coffee in blender container; cover. Blend on medium speed until smooth. Add pudding mixes and remaining 2 cups milk; cover. Blend on medium speed until smooth. Carefully pour into prepared bowl. Top with whipped topping.

REFRIGERATE at least 3 hours or until set. Just before serving, sprinkle with additional undissolved flavored instant coffee, if desired. *Makes 12 servings*

Philadelphia® Cinnamon Orange Spread

Prep Time: 5 minutes

1 **package (8 ounces) PHILADELPHIA® Cream Cheese, softened**
½ **cup orange marmalade**
Ground cinnamon

SPREAD cream cheese on serving plate.

TOP with orange marmalade; sprinkle with cinnamon. Serve with gingersnaps or vanilla wafers. *Makes 10 servings*

Gift Box

1 package (12 ounces) pound cake
1 package (8 ounces) PHILADELPHIA® Cream Cheese, cubed, softened
1½ cups cold milk, divided
1 package (4-serving size) JELL-O® Lemon or Vanilla Flavor Instant
    Pudding & Pie Filling
1 teaspoon grated lemon peel
1 tub (8 ounces) COOL WHIP® Whipped Topping, thawed
1 can (11 ounces) mandarin orange segments, drained
    Chewy fruit snack rolls
    Assorted small candies

LINE bottom and sides of 8×4-inch loaf pan with wax paper.

CUT rounded top off cake; reserve for snacking or another use. Trim edges of cake. Cut cake horizontally into 5 slices. Line bottom and long sides of pan with 3 cake slices. Cut another cake slice crosswise in half; place on short sides of pan.

BEAT cream cheese and ½ cup of the milk in large bowl with electric mixer on low speed until smooth. Add remaining milk, pudding mix and lemon peel. Beat 1 to 2 minutes or until well blended. Gently stir in 1 cup of the whipped topping and oranges. Spoon filling into cake-lined pan. Place remaining cake slice on top of filling.

REFRIGERATE 3 hours or until firm. Invert pan onto serving plate; remove pan and wax paper. Frost top and sides of cake with remaining whipped topping. Decorate with snack roll to form ribbon. Garnish with candies.   *Makes 16 servings*

Chocolate "Ornaments"

1 package (8 squares) BAKER'S® Semi-Sweet Chocolate
½ package (4 ounces) PHILADELPHIA® Cream Cheese, cubed, softened
1 tub (8 ounces) COOL WHIP® Whipped Topping, thawed
    Assorted coatings, such as: powdered sugar, finely chopped nuts,
      toasted BAKER'S® ANGEL FLAKE Coconut, grated BAKER'S®
      Semi-Sweet Chocolate, cookie crumbs or multicolored sprinkles

MICROWAVE chocolate in large microwavable bowl on HIGH 2 minutes or until chocolate is almost melted, stirring halfway through heating time. Stir until chocolate is completely melted. Add cream cheese; stir with wire whisk until smooth. Cool 20 minutes or until room temperature. Gently stir in whipped topping with wire whisk until blended.

FREEZE 1 hour; scoop into 1-inch balls. If necessary, freeze balls 30 minutes longer or until firm enough to roll. Roll in assorted coatings as desired. Refrigerate or freeze until ready to serve.   *Makes 2½ to 3 dozen*

Top to bottom: Gift Box and Chocolate "Ornaments"

Cherry Cheesecake Squares

Prep Time: 20 minutes plus refrigerating   *Bake Time:* 45 minutes

> 2 cups graham cracker crumbs
> ¼ cup sugar
> ¼ cup (½ stick) butter or margarine, melted
> 3 packages (8 ounces each) PHILADELPHIA® Cream Cheese, softened
> ¾ cup sugar
> 1 teaspoon vanilla
> 2 eggs
> 1 can (20 ounces) cherry pie filling

MIX crumbs, ¼ cup sugar and butter. Press into 13×9-inch baking pan. Bake at 325°F for 10 minutes.

MIX cream cheese, ¾ cup sugar and vanilla with electric mixer on medium speed until well blended. Add eggs; mix just until blended. Pour over crust.

BAKE at 325°F for 35 minutes or until center is almost set. Cool. Refrigerate 3 hours or overnight. Top with pie filling. Cut into squares.   *Makes 18 servings*

Chocolate Fudge

Prep Time: 15 minutes plus refrigerating

> 4 cups sifted powdered sugar
> 1 package (8 ounces) PHILADELPHIA® Cream Cheese, softened
> 4 squares BAKER'S® Unsweetened Chocolate, melted
> ½ cup chopped nuts
> 1 teaspoon vanilla

ADD sugar gradually to cream cheese, beating with electric mixer on medium speed until well blended. Add remaining ingredients; mix well.

SPREAD into greased 8-inch square pan. Refrigerate several hours.

CUT into 1-inch squares.   *Makes 64 squares*

Peppermint Fudge: Omit nuts and vanilla. Add few drops peppermint extract and ¼ cup crushed peppermint candies. Sprinkle with additional ¼ cup crushed peppermint candies before refrigerating.

Coconut Fudge: Omit nuts. Add 1 cup BAKER'S® ANGEL FLAKE® Coconut. Garnish with additional coconut.

Cappuccino Cream

1 package (8 ounces) PHILADELPHIA® Cream Cheese, softened
1 cup brewed strong MAXWELL HOUSE® Coffee, at room temperature
½ cup milk
1 package (4-serving size) JELL-O® Brand Vanilla Flavor Instant Pudding & Pie Filling
¼ teaspoon ground cinnamon
1 tub (8 ounces) COOL WHIP® Whipped Topping, thawed, divided
   Cookies, such as chocolate-laced pirouettes *or* biscotti

MIX cream cheese with electric mixer on medium speed until smooth. Gradually add coffee and milk, beating until well blended. Add pudding mix and cinnamon. Beat on low speed 2 minutes. Let stand 5 minutes or until thickened.

STIR in 2 cups whipped topping. Spoon into 6 dessert glasses or 1-quart serving bowl.

REFRIGERATE until ready to serve. Just before serving, top with remaining whipped topping. Serve with cookies.   *Makes 6 servings*

Chocolate Candy Bar Dessert

2 cups chocolate wafer cookie crumbs
½ cup sugar, divided
½ cup (1 stick) butter or margarine, melted
1 package (8 ounces) PHILADELPHIA® Cream Cheese, softened
1 tub (12 ounces) COOL WHIP® Whipped Topping, thawed
1 cup chopped chocolate-covered candy bars
3 cups cold milk
2 packages (4-serving size) JELL-O® Chocolate Flavor Instant Pudding & Pie Filling

MIX cookie crumbs, ¼ cup of the sugar and butter in 13×9-inch pan. Press firmly onto bottom of pan. Refrigerate until ready to fill.

BEAT cream cheese and remaining ¼ cup sugar in medium bowl with wire whisk until smooth. Gently stir in ½ of the whipped topping. Spread evenly over crust. Sprinkle chopped candy bars over cream cheese layer.

POUR milk into large bowl. Add pudding mixes. Beat with wire whisk 1 minute. Pour over chopped candy bar layer. Let stand 5 minutes or until thickened. Spread remaining whipped topping over pudding layer.

REFRIGERATE 2 hours or until set.   *Makes 15 servings*

Cherries in the Snow

Prep Time: 10 minutes

> **1 package (8 ounces) PHILADELPHIA® Cream Cheese, softened**
> **½ cup sugar**
> **2 cups COOL WHIP® Whipped Topping, thawed**
> **1 can (20 ounces) cherry pie filling, divided**

MIX cream cheese and sugar in large bowl until smooth. Gently stir in whipped topping.

LAYER ¼ cup cream cheese mixture and 2 tablespoons pie filling in each of 4 stemmed glasses or bowls. Repeat layers.   *Makes 4 servings*

Peachy Berry Dessert

Prep Time: 15 minutes

> **½ cup plus 1 tablespoon sugar**
> **½ teaspoon ground cinnamon**
> **½ package (15 ounces) refrigerated pie crust**
> **1 tablespoon butter *or* margarine, melted**
> **2 cans (15 ounces each) peach slices in juice**
> **2 packages (8 ounces each) PHILADELPHIA® Cream Cheese, softened**
> **1 tub (12 ounces) COOL WHIP® Whipped Topping, thawed**
> **½ cup blueberries**

HEAT oven to 400°F.

STIR 1 tablespoon sugar and cinnamon together in small bowl. Unfold crust; cut into 10 to 12 wedges. Place pastry wedges on cookie sheet, ½ inch apart. Brush with melted butter and sprinkle with sugar mixture. Bake 8 to 10 minutes or until lightly browned. Remove to wire rack; cool.

DRAIN peaches, reserving ½ cup juice. Beat cream cheese and remaining ½ cup sugar in large bowl with wire whisk until smooth. Gradually beat in reserved juice. Fold in 4½ cups whipped topping. Spoon into shallow bowl. Top with remaining whipped topping, peaches and blueberries.

ARRANGE pastry wedges in pinwheel fashion on top.

Makes 10 to 12 servings

Variation: 3 cups fresh sliced peaches and ½ cup peach nectar may be substituted for canned peaches.

Holiday Peppermint Candies

Prep Time: 30 minutes plus refrigerating

½ **package (4 ounces) PHILADELPHIA® Cream Cheese, softened**
1 **tablespoon butter** *or* **margarine**
1 **tablespoon light corn syrup**
¼ **teaspoon peppermint extract** *or* **few drops peppermint oil**
4 **cups powdered sugar**
  Green and red food coloring
  Sifted powdered sugar
  Green, red and white decorating icing (optional)

MIX cream cheese, butter, corn syrup and extract in large mixing bowl with electric mixer on medium speed until well blended. Gradually add 4 cups powdered sugar; mix well.

DIVIDE mixture into thirds. Knead a few drops green food coloring into first third; repeat with red food coloring and second third. Wrap each third in plastic wrap.

SHAPE into 1-inch balls, working with 1 color mixture at a time. Place on wax paper-lined cookie sheet. Flatten each ball with bottom of glass that has been lightly dipped in sifted powdered sugar.

REPEAT with remaining mixtures. Decorate with icing. Store candies in refrigerator.

Makes 5 dozen

Tip

Before measuring out corn syrup, lightly coat the measuring spoon with nonstick cooking spray. The corn syrup will slide right out and cleanup will be a breeze.

142

Brownie Pizza

Prep Time: 30 minutes   *Bake Time:* 40 minutes

Brownie Layer
4 squares BAKER'S® Unsweetened Chocolate
¾ cup (1½ sticks) margarine or butter
2 cups sugar
4 eggs
1 teaspoon vanilla
1 cup all-purpose flour

Topping
1 package (8 ounces) PHILADELPHIA® Cream Cheese, softened
¼ cup sugar
1 egg
½ teaspoon vanilla
Assorted sliced fruit
2 squares BAKER'S® Semi-Sweet Chocolate, melted

HEAT oven to 350°F. Line 12×½-inch pizza pan with foil (to lift brownie from pan after baking); grease foil.

MICROWAVE unsweetened chocolate and margarine in large microwavable bowl on HIGH 2 minutes or until margarine is melted. **Stir until chocolate is completely melted.**

STIR 2 cups sugar into melted chocolate mixture. Mix in 4 eggs and 1 teaspoon vanilla until well blended. Stir in flour. Spread in prepared pan. Bake for 30 minutes.

MIX cream cheese, ¼ cup sugar, 1 egg and ½ teaspoon vanilla in same bowl until well blended. Pour over baked brownie crust.

BAKE 10 minutes longer or until toothpick inserted into center comes out with fudgy crumbs. **Do not overbake.** Cool in pan. Lift brownie pizza out of pan; peel off foil. Place brownie pizza on serving plate. Arrange fruit over cream cheese layer. Drizzle with melted semi-sweet chocolate.

Makes 12 servings

145

Cakes & Pies

Lemon Berry Pie

½ package (4 ounces) PHILADELPHIA® Cream Cheese, cubed, softened
1 tablespoon milk
1 tablespoon sugar
2 teaspoons grated lemon peel
1 tablespoon fresh lemon juice
1 tub (8 ounces) COOL WHIP® Whipped Topping, thawed
1 ready-to-use graham cracker crumb crust (6 ounces or 9 inch)
1 pint strawberries
2 cups cold milk
2 packages (4-serving size) JELL-O® Vanilla or Lemon Flavor Instant Pudding & Pie Filling

BEAT cream cheese, 1 tablespoon milk and sugar in medium bowl with wire whisk until smooth. Stir in lemon peel and juice. Gently stir in 1½ cups of the whipped topping. Spread evenly onto bottom of crust. Reserve a few strawberries for garnish, if desired; cut remaining strawberries in half. Press strawberry halves into cream cheese layer.

POUR 2 cups milk into large bowl. Add pudding mixes. Beat with wire whisk 1 minute. Gently stir in 1 cup of the whipped topping. Spoon over strawberries in crust.

REFRIGERATE 4 hours or until set. Garnish with remaining whipped topping and reserved strawberries just before serving. *Makes 8 servings*

Cool Tips: To soften cream cheese, place unwrapped package of cream cheese on microwavable plate. Microwave on HIGH 15 to 20 seconds.

Carrot Cake with Easy Cream Cheese Frosting

Prep Time: 20 minutes

    1 package (2-layer size) carrot cake mix
    1 package (8 ounces) PHILADELPHIA® Cream Cheese, softened
    $\frac{1}{3}$ cup granulated *or* powdered sugar
    $\frac{1}{4}$ cup cold milk
    1 tub (8 ounces) COOL WHIP® Whipped Topping, thawed

PREPARE cake mix as directed on package for 13×9-inch pan. Cool completely.

BEAT cream cheese, sugar and milk in medium bowl with wire whisk until smooth. Gently stir in whipped topping. Spread over top of cake.

REFRIGERATE until ready to serve. Garnish as desired.   *Makes 10 servings*

Note: Substitute your favorite carrot cake recipe for carrot cake mix.

Fluffy Lemon Fruit Pie

Prep Time: 10 minutes

    1 can (21 ounces) cherry pie filling
    1 ready-to-use graham cracker crumb crust (6 ounces or 9 inch)
    1 package (8 ounces) PHILADELPHIA® Cream Cheese, softened
    1 cup cold milk
    1 package (4-serving size) JELL-O® Lemon Flavor Instant Pudding
       & Pie Filling
    1 tub (8 ounces) COOL WHIP® Whipped Topping, thawed

SPREAD half of the cherry pie filling on bottom of crust.

BEAT cream cheese in large bowl with wire whisk until smooth. Gradually beat in milk until well blended. Add pudding mix. Beat until smooth. Gently stir in half of the whipped topping. Spread over pie filling.

SPREAD remaining whipped topping over pudding mixture. Spoon remaining cherry pie filling over whipped topping layer.

REFRIGERATE 3 hours or until set. Garnish as desired.   *Makes 8 servings*

German Sweet Chocolate Pie

1 package (4 ounces) BAKER'S® GERMAN'S® Sweet Chocolate
⅓ cup milk, divided
½ package (4 ounces) PHILADELPHIA® Cream Cheese, cubed, softened
2 tablespoons sugar
1 tub (8 ounces) COOL WHIP® Whipped Topping, thawed
1 ready-to-use graham cracker crumb crust (6 ounces or 9 inch)
   Additional COOL WHIP® Whipped Topping, thawed
   Shaved chocolate

MICROWAVE chocolate and 2 tablespoons of the milk in large microwavable bowl on HIGH 1½ to 2 minutes or until chocolate is almost melted, stirring halfway through heating time. Stir until chocolate is completely melted.

BEAT cream cheese, sugar and remaining milk into chocolate with wire whisk until well blended. Refrigerate about 10 minutes to cool. Gently stir in 1 tub whipped topping until smooth. Spoon into crust.

FREEZE 4 hours or until firm. Let stand at room temperature 15 minutes before serving or until pie can be cut easily. Garnish with additional whipped topping and shaved chocolate.

Makes 8 servings

Tip

German's Sweet Chocolate is a special blend of chocolate; it is enriched with cocoa butter and sugar and retains its rich and mild flavor in recipes.

Apple Cranberry Pie

Prep Time: 15 minutes plus cooling   *Bake Time:* 45 minutes

  1 package (8 ounces) PHILADELPHIA® Cream Cheese, softened
  ½ cup firmly packed brown sugar, divided
  1 egg
  1 (9-inch) unbaked pastry shell
  2 cups sliced apples
  ½ cup halved cranberries
  1 teaspoon ground cinnamon, divided
  ⅓ cup flour
  ⅓ cup old-fashioned or quick-cooking oats, uncooked
  ¼ cup (½ stick) butter or margarine
  ¼ cup chopped nuts

MIX cream cheese and ¼ cup of the sugar with electric mixer on medium speed until well blended. Blend in egg. Pour into pastry shell.

TOSS apples, cranberries and ½ teaspoon cinnamon. Spoon over cream cheese mixture.

MIX flour, oats, remaining ¼ cup sugar and remaining ½ teaspoon cinnamon. Cut in butter until mixture resembles coarse crumbs. Stir in nuts. Spoon over fruit mixture.

BAKE at 375°F for 40 to 45 minutes or until lightly browned. Cool slightly before serving.   *Makes 8 to 10 servings*

Creamy Orange Cake

1 can (6 ounces) frozen orange juice concentrate, thawed
1 package (2-layer size) yellow cake mix
1 package (3 ounces) PHILADELPHIA® Cream Cheese, softened
¼ cup sugar
1 tub (12 ounces) COOL WHIP® Whipped Topping, thawed
Mandarin orange sections (optional)
Fresh mint leaves (optional)

POUR concentrate into 2-cup measuring cup, reserving 2 tablespoons for cake filling. Add enough water to remaining concentrate to make the amount of liquid needed for cake mix. Prepare cake mix as directed on package, using measured liquid. Pour into 2 greased and floured 9-inch round cake pans. Bake and cool as directed on package.

BEAT cream cheese and sugar in large bowl with electric mixer on low speed until smooth. Beat in reserved concentrate. Gently stir in ½ cup of the whipped topping.

PLACE 1 cake layer on serving plate. Spread with cream cheese mixture. Top with second cake layer. Frost cake with remaining whipped topping. Dollop additional whipped topping around bottom of cake, if desired. Garnish with orange sections and mint leaves. Store cake in refrigerator. *Makes 12 to 16 servings*

Father's Day Cheesecake Pie

1 package (8 ounces) PHILADELPHIA® Cream Cheese, softened
⅓ cup sugar
1 teaspoon vanilla
1 tub (8 ounces) COOL WHIP® Whipped Topping, thawed
1 ready-to-use graham cracker crumb crust (6 ounces or 9 inch)
Additional COOL WHIP® Whipped Topping (about ½ cup), thawed
KRAFT® Miniature Marshmallows
Strawberry dessert topping or jam

BEAT cream cheese, sugar and vanilla with wire whisk in large bowl until smooth. Gently stir in whipped topping. Spoon into crust.

REFRIGERATE at least 4 hours or until set.

DECORATE top of pie with additional whipped topping and marshmallows to resemble a tie. Fill in tie and outline edge of pie with dessert topping. Store leftover pie in refrigerator. *Makes 8 servings*

Cream Cheese Brownie Pie

Prep Time: 30 minutes   *Bake Time:* 45 minutes

½ package (15 ounces) refrigerated pie crust
1 package (8 ounces) PHILADELPHIA® Cream Cheese, softened
¼ cup sugar
3 eggs, divided
6 squares BAKER'S® Semi-Sweet Baking Chocolate
½ cup (1 stick) butter *or* margarine
⅔ cup sugar
1 teaspoon vanilla
1 cup flour
2 squares BAKER'S® Semi-Sweet Baking Chocolate, melted (optional)

HEAT oven to 350°F. Prepare crust as directed on package, using 9-inch pie plate. Mix cream cheese, ¼ cup sugar and 1 egg in medium bowl until well blended; set aside.

MICROWAVE chocolate and butter in large microwavable bowl on HIGH 2 minutes or until butter is melted. Stir until chocolate is completely melted.

STIR ⅔ cup sugar into chocolate mixture until well blended. Mix in 2 eggs and vanilla. Stir in flour until well blended. Spread half of the brownie batter into prepared crust. Carefully spread cream cheese mixture over top. Top with remaining brownie batter.

BAKE 45 minutes or until toothpick inserted in center comes out with fudgy crumbs. Cool completely on wire rack. Drizzle with melted chocolate, if desired.

Makes 10 servings

To soften cream cheese in the microwave: Place 1 completely unwrapped (8-ounce) package of cream cheese in microwavable bowl. Microwave on HIGH 15 seconds. Add 15 seconds for each additional package of cream cheese.

Layer After Layer Lemon Pie

Prep Time: 20 minutes   *Refrigerating Time:* 4 hours

⅓ cup strawberry jam
1 ready-to-use graham cracker or shortbread crumb crust (6 ounces or 9 inch)
4 ounces PHILADELPHIA® Cream Cheese, softened
1 tablespoon sugar
1 tub (8 ounces) COOL WHIP® Whipped Topping, thawed, divided
1½ cups cold milk or half-and-half
2 packages (4-serving size each) JELL-O® Lemon Flavor Instant Pudding & Pie Filling
2 teaspoons grated lemon peel

SPREAD jam gently onto bottom of pie crust. Mix cream cheese and sugar in large bowl with wire whisk until smooth. Gently stir in ½ of the whipped topping. Spread on top of jam.

POUR milk into large bowl. Add pudding mixes and lemon peel. Beat with wire whisk 1 minute. (Mixture will be thick.) Gently stir in remaining whipped topping. Spread over cream cheese layer.

REFRIGERATE 4 hours or until set. Garnish with additional whipped topping, if desired.   ***Makes 8 servings***

Best of the Season: For an extra-special fruity flavor, place 1 cup strawberries into jam on bottom of crust; proceed as above.

Take a Shortcut: Soften cream cheese in microwave on HIGH 15 to 20 seconds.

Chocolate-Chocolate Cake

Prep Time: 10 minutes plus cooling   *Bake Time:* 1 hour 5 minutes

1 package (8 ounces) PHILADELPHIA® Cream Cheese, softened
1 cup BREAKSTONE'S® *or* KNUDSEN® Sour Cream
½ cup coffee-flavored liqueur *or* water
2 eggs
1 package (2-layer size) chocolate cake mix
1 package (4-serving size) JELL-O® Chocolate Flavor Instant Pudding
**   & Pie Filling**
1 cup BAKER'S® Semi-Sweet Real Chocolate Chips

MIX cream cheese, sour cream, liqueur and eggs with electric mixer on medium speed until well blended. Add cake mix and pudding mix; beat until well blended. Fold in chips. (Batter will be stiff.)

POUR into greased and floured 12-cup fluted tube pan.

BAKE at 325°F for 1 hour to 1 hour and 5 minutes or until toothpick inserted near center comes out clean. Cool 5 minutes. Remove from pan. Cool completely on wire rack. Sprinkle with powdered sugar before serving. Garnish, if desired.

Makes 10 to 12 servings

> **Tip**
>
> Eggs and other ingredients for cakes should
> be at room temperature before mixing. This
> will result in better volume from cakes than
> using cold ingredients.

Cheesecake Garden Tarts

¼ cup strawberry or apricot preserves
10 prepared graham cracker crumb tart shells
 1 package (8 ounces) PHILADELPHIA® Cream Cheese
⅓ cup sugar
 1 teaspoon vanilla
 1 tub (8 ounces) COOL WHIP® Whipped Topping, thawed
 Sliced almonds
 Assorted berries and sliced fresh fruits
 Hot fudge topping
 Fresh mint leaves

SPREAD preserves onto bottom of tart shells. Beat cream cheese, sugar and vanilla in large bowl with wire whisk until smooth. Gently stir in whipped topping. Spoon evenly into tart shells.

REFRIGERATE 2 hours or until set. Decorate with almonds, fruits and topping to resemble flowers. Arrange on serving plate. Garnish with mint leaves.

Makes 10 tarts

Tip

These tarts are perfect for entertaining and can be made a day ahead if left plain. The fruit and toppings should be added close to serving time so they do not cause the tarts to become soggy.

Chocolate Peppermint Pie

1 cup crushed chocolate-covered mint-flavored cookies
3 tablespoons hot water
1 ready-to-use graham cracker crumb crust (6 ounces or 9 inch)
½ package (4 ounces) PHILADELPHIA® Cream Cheese, softened
⅓ cup sugar
2 tablespoons milk
¼ teaspoon peppermint extract
1 tub (8 ounces) COOL WHIP® Whipped Topping, thawed
6 to 10 drops green food coloring
   Additional thawed COOL WHIP® Whipped Topping
   Green gumdrop spearmint leaves (optional)
   Red cinnamon candies (optional)

MIX cookies and hot water in small bowl. Spread evenly on bottom of crust.

BEAT cream cheese in large bowl with electric mixer on medium speed until smooth. Gradually beat in sugar, milk and peppermint extract until well blended. Gently stir in whipped topping. Divide mixture in half; stir food coloring into ½ of the whipped topping mixture until evenly colored. Spoon green and white whipped topping mixtures alternately into crust. Smooth top with spatula.

REFRIGERATE 3 hours or until set. Garnish with additional whipped topping before serving. Decorate with spearmint leaves and cinnamon candies to make holly leaves and berries. Store leftover pie in refrigerator.   *Makes 8 servings*

Pumpkin Orange Double Layer Pie

Prep Time: 20 minutes plus refrigerating

4 ounces PHILADELPHIA® Cream Cheese, softened
⅓ cup orange marmalade
1½ cups thawed COOL WHIP® Whipped Topping
1 ready-to-use graham cracker crumb crust (6 ounces or 9 inch)
¾ cup cold milk *or* half-and-half
2 packages (4-serving size each) JELL-O® Vanilla Flavor Instant Pudding & Pie Filling
1 can (16 ounces) pumpkin
1 teaspoon pumpkin pie spice

MIX cream cheese and marmalade in large bowl with wire whisk until smooth. Stir in whipped topping. Spread on bottom of crust.

POUR milk into large bowl. Add pudding mixes, pumpkin and spice. Beat with wire whisk 2 minutes or until well blended. Spread over cream cheese layer. Refrigerate 4 hours or until set. Garnish with additional whipped topping.

Makes 8 servings

Better-Than-S_x Cake

Prep Time: 30 minutes   *Refrigerating Time:* 2 hours

1½ cups graham cracker crumbs
⅔ cup chopped pecans, divided
½ cup (1 stick) butter or margarine, melted
6 tablespoons sugar
1 package (8 ounces) PHILADELPHIA® Cream Cheese, softened
3½ cups cold milk
2 packages (4-serving size) JELL-O® Vanilla Flavor Instant Pudding & Pie Filling
1⅓ cups BAKER'S® ANGEL FLAKE® Coconut, divided
1 tub (8 ounces) COOL WHIP® Whipped Topping, thawed

MIX crumbs, ⅓ cup pecans, butter and sugar in 13×9-inch pan. Press firmly onto bottom of pan.

BEAT cream cheese in large bowl with electric mixer on low speed until smooth. Gradually beat in ½ cup milk. Add remaining milk and pudding mix. Beat on low speed about 2 minutes or until well blended. Stir in 1 cup coconut. Pour immediately over crust. Spread whipped topping evenly over pudding mixture.

REFRIGERATE 2 hours or until set. Toast remaining ⅓ cup coconut and ⅓ cup pecans. Sprinkle over top of dessert.

Makes 15 servings

Chilled Lemon Pie

Prep Time: 20 minutes plus refrigerating

    1 **envelope unflavored gelatin**
   ¼ **cup lemon juice**
    2 **packages (8 ounces each) PHILADELPHIA® Cream Cheese, softened**
   ½ **cup sugar**
    1 **container (8 ounces) lemon yogurt**
   ½ **teaspoon grated lemon peel**
    1 **cup whipping cream, whipped**
    1 **(9-inch) baked pastry shell**
     Currant Raspberry Sauce (recipe follows)

SPRINKLE gelatin over juice in small saucepan. Let stand 5 minutes to soften. Cook and stir on low heat until gelatin is completely dissolved. Do not boil.

MIX cream cheese and sugar with electric mixer on medium speed until well blended. Blend in yogurt and peel. Stir in gelatin. Refrigerate until mixture is slightly thickened, but not set.

FOLD in whipped cream. Spoon into crust. Refrigerate several hours or overnight until firm. Serve with sauce.   *Makes 8 to 10 servings*

Currant Raspberry Sauce

    1 **package (10 ounces) frozen red raspberries, thawed**
   ½ **cup red currant jelly**
    4 **teaspoons cornstarch**

PLACE raspberries and jelly in food processor fitted with steel blade or blender container; cover. Process until well blended. Strain.

STIR cornstarch and raspberry mixture in small saucepan until smooth. Bring to boil on medium heat, stirring constantly. Cook until thickened, stirring constantly. Cool. Serve with pie.

Cookies & Bars

Creamy Lemon Bars

Prep Time: 15 minutes   *Bake Time:* 35 minutes

1 package (2-layer size) lemon cake mix
3 large eggs, divided
½ cup oil
2 packages (8 ounces each) PHILADELPHIA® Cream Cheese, softened
1 container (8 ounces) BREAKSTONE'S® *or* KNUDSEN® Sour Cream
½ cup granulated sugar
1 teaspoon grated lemon peel
1 tablespoon lemon juice
   Powdered sugar

MIX cake mix, 1 egg and oil. Press mixture onto bottom and up sides of lightly greased 15×10×1-inch baking pan. Bake at 350°F for 10 minutes.

BEAT cream cheese with electric mixer on medium speed until smooth. Add remaining 2 eggs, sour cream, granulated sugar, peel and juice; mix until blended. Pour batter into crust.

BAKE at 350°F for 30 to 35 minutes or until filling is just set in center and edges are light golden brown. Cool. Sprinkle with powdered sugar. Cut into bars. Store leftover bars in refrigerator.   *Makes 2 dozen*

Philadelphia® Sugar Cookies

Prep Time: 10 minutes plus refrigerating   *Bake Time:* 15 minutes

- **1 package (8 ounces) PHILADELPHIA® Cream Cheese, softened**
- **1 cup (2 sticks) butter *or* margarine, softened**
- **⅔ cup sugar**
- **¼ teaspoon vanilla**
- **2 cups flour**
- **Colored sugar, sprinkles and colored gels**

BEAT cream cheese, butter, ⅔ cup sugar and vanilla with electric mixer on medium speed until well blended. Mix in flour. Refrigerate several hours or overnight.

ROLL dough to ¼-inch thickness on lightly floured surface. Cut into desired shapes; sprinkle with colored sugar. Place on ungreased cookie sheets.

BAKE at 350°F for 12 to 15 minutes or until edges are lightly browned. Cool on wire racks. Decorate as desired with colored sugar, sprinkles and colored gels.

Makes 3½ dozen

Chocolate Peanut Butter Bars

Prep Time: 20 minutes   *Bake Time:* 20 minutes

- **1½ cups chocolate-covered graham cracker crumbs (about 17 crackers)**
- **3 tablespoons butter *or* margarine, melted**
- **1 package (8 ounces) PHILADELPHIA® Cream Cheese, softened**
- **½ cup crunchy peanut butter**
- **1 cup powdered sugar**
- **2 squares BAKER'S® Semi-Sweet Baking Chocolate**
- **1 teaspoon butter *or* margarine**

MIX crumbs and 3 tablespoons melted butter. Press onto bottom of 9-inch square baking pan. Bake at 350°F for 20 minutes. Cool.

BEAT cream cheese, peanut butter and sugar with electric mixer on medium speed until well blended. Spoon over crust.

MICROWAVE chocolate with 1 teaspoon butter on HIGH 1 to 2 minutes or until chocolate begins to melt, stirring halfway through heating time. Stir until chocolate is completely melted. Drizzle over cream cheese mixture.

REFRIGERATE 6 hours or overnight. Cut into squares. Store in airtight container in refrigerator.

Makes 18 servings

Cappuccino Bars

Prep Time: 10 minutes

  15 whole chocolate graham crackers, divided
  2 packages (8 ounces each) PHILADELPHIA® Cream Cheese, softened
3½ cups cold milk
  3 packages (4-serving size each) JELL-O® Chocolate Flavor Instant
       Pudding & Pie Filling
  1 tablespoon MAXWELL HOUSE® Instant Coffee
¼ teaspoon ground cinnamon
  1 tub (8 ounces) COOL WHIP® Whipped Topping, thawed
  1 square BAKER'S® Semi-Sweet Baking Chocolate, grated *or*
       3 tablespoons chocolate sprinkles

ARRANGE half of the crackers in bottom of 13×9-inch pan, cutting crackers to fit, if necessary.

BEAT cream cheese in large bowl with electric mixer on low speed until smooth. Gradually beat in 1 cup milk. Add remaining milk, pudding mixes, instant coffee and cinnamon. Beat 1 to 2 minutes. (Mixture will be thick.) Gently stir in 2 cups whipped topping.

SPREAD half of the pudding mixture over crackers in pan. Arrange remaining crackers over pudding in pan. Top with remaining pudding mixture. Cover with remaining whipped topping. Sprinkle with grated chocolate.

FREEZE 3 hours or overnight. Cut into bars. Garnish as desired.

Makes 18 servings

Almond Macaroon Brownies

Brownie Layer

> 6 squares BAKER'S® Semi-Sweet Chocolate
> ½ cup (1 stick) margarine or butter
> ⅔ cup sugar
> 2 eggs
> 1 teaspoon vanilla
> 1 cup all-purpose flour
> ⅓ cup chopped toasted almonds

Cream Cheese Topping

> ½ package (4 ounces) PHILADELPHIA® Cream Cheese, softened
> ⅓ cup sugar
> 1 egg
> 1 tablespoon all-purpose flour
> ⅓ cup chopped toasted almonds
> 1 cup BAKER'S® ANGEL FLAKE® Coconut
>   Whole almonds (optional)
> 1 square BAKER'S® Semi-Sweet Chocolate, melted (optional)

PREHEAT oven to 350°F.

MICROWAVE 6 squares chocolate and margarine in large microwavable bowl on HIGH (100% power) 2 minutes or until margarine is melted. Stir until chocolate is completely melted.

STIR ⅔ cup sugar into melted chocolate mixture. Mix in 2 eggs and vanilla until well blended. Stir in 1 cup flour and ⅓ cup chopped almonds. Spread in greased 8-inch square pan.

MIX cream cheese, ⅓ cup sugar, 1 egg and 1 tablespoon flour in small bowl until smooth. Stir in ⅓ cup chopped almonds and coconut. Spread over brownie batter. Garnish with whole almonds, if desired.

BAKE for 35 minutes or until wooden toothpick inserted into center comes out with fudgy crumbs. Do not overbake. Cool in pan on wire rack. Drizzle with 1 square melted chocolate, if desired. Cool until chocolate is set. Cut into squares.

Makes about 16 brownies

Praline Bars

¾ cup butter or margarine, softened
1 cup sugar, divided
1 teaspoon vanilla, divided
1½ cups flour
2 packages (8 ounces each) PHILADELPHIA® Cream Cheese, softened
2 eggs
½ cup almond brickle chips
3 tablespoons caramel ice cream topping

MIX butter, ½ cup of the sugar and ½ teaspoon of the vanilla with electric mixer on medium speed until light and fluffy. Gradually add flour, mixing on low speed until blended. Press onto bottom of 13×9-inch pan. Bake at 350°F for 20 to 23 minutes or until lightly browned.

MIX cream cheese, remaining ½ cup sugar and ½ teaspoon vanilla with electric mixer on medium speed until well blended. Add eggs; mix well. Blend in chips. Pour over crust. Dot top of cream cheese mixture with topping. Cut through batter with knife several times for marble effect.

BAKE at 350°F for 30 minutes. Cool in pan on wire rack. Cut into bars.

Makes 2 dozen bars

Fudgy Nut Squares

1 cup (2 sticks) butter *or* margarine, divided
1 cup BAKER'S® Semi-Sweet Real Chocolate Chips, divided
1¾ cups graham cracker crumbs
1 cup BAKER'S® ANGEL FLAKE® Coconut
½ cup chopped nuts
1 package (8 ounces) PHILADELPHIA® Cream Cheese, softened
½ cup sugar
1 teaspoon vanilla

STIR ¾ cup of the butter and ⅓ cup of the chips in saucepan on low heat until smooth. Mix cracker crumbs, coconut and nuts. Stir into butter mixture in saucepan. Press onto bottom of ungreased 15×10×1-inch baking pan. Refrigerate 30 minutes or until firm.

MIX cream cheese, sugar and vanilla with electric mixer on medium speed until well blended. Spread over crust. Refrigerate 30 minutes or until firm.

MELT remaining ¼ cup butter and ½ cup chips; spread over cream cheese layer. Refrigerate until firm. Cut into squares. *Makes about 24 squares*

Banana Split Cheesecake Squares

Prep Time: 20 minutes plus refrigerating   *Bake Time:* 30 minutes

Crust

2 cups graham cracker crumbs
⅓ cup butter *or* margarine, melted
¼ cup sugar

Filling

3 packages (8 ounces each) PHILADELPHIA® Cream Cheese, softened
¾ cup sugar
1 teaspoon vanilla
3 eggs
½ cup mashed ripe banana

Topping

1 banana, sliced
1 teaspoon lemon juice
1 cup halved strawberries
1 can (8 ounces) pineapple chunks, drained
Chopped nuts (optional)
BAKER'S® Semi-Sweet Baking Chocolate, melted (optional)

Crust

MIX crumbs, butter and sugar. Press onto bottom of 13×9-inch baking pan.

Filling

MIX cream cheese, sugar and vanilla with electric mixer on medium speed until well blended. Add eggs; mix until blended. Stir in mashed banana. Pour over crust. Bake at 350°F for 30 minutes or until center is almost set. Cool. Refrigerate 3 hours or overnight.

Topping

TOSS banana with lemon juice. Mix in strawberries and pineapple. Spoon evenly over cheesecake. Sprinkle with nuts and drizzle with chocolate. Cut into squares. Refrigerate any leftover cheesecake.

Makes 2 dozen squares

Choco-Cherry Bars

Prep Time: 30 minutes   *Bake Time:* 30 minutes

Bars

　1 package (8 ounces) PHILADELPHIA® Cream Cheese, softened
¾ cup (1½ sticks) butter *or* margarine, softened
　1 cup sugar
　2 eggs
　1 teaspoon vanilla
1¼ cups flour
½ teaspoon *each* baking soda and salt
　2 squares BAKER'S® Unsweetened Baking Chocolate, melted
　1 cup chopped maraschino cherries, well drained
½ cup chopped walnuts

Glaze

　1 cup sifted powdered sugar
　3 tablespoons milk
　2 squares BAKER'S® Unsweetened Baking Chocolate, melted
½ teaspoon vanilla

Bars

MIX cream cheese, butter and sugar with electric mixer on medium speed until well blended. Add eggs and vanilla; mix until blended.

MIX flour, baking soda and salt. Add flour mixture to cream cheese mixture; mix well. Blend in melted chocolate. Stir in cherries and walnuts. Spread into greased and floured 15×10×1-inch baking pan.

BAKE at 350°F for 25 to 30 minutes or until toothpick inserted in center comes out clean.

Glaze

MIX powdered sugar, milk, melted chocolate and vanilla until smooth. Drizzle over warm bars in baking pan; cut into bars.　　　　　***Makes 2 dozen bars***

Philadelphia® Snowmen Cookies

Prep Time: 20 minutes   *Bake Time:* 21 minutes

> **1 package (8 ounces) PHILADELPHIA® Cream Cheese, softened**
> **1 cup powdered sugar**
> **¾ cup (1½ sticks) butter *or* margarine**
> **½ teaspoon vanilla**
> **2¼ cups flour**
> **½ teaspoon baking soda**
> **Sifted powdered sugar**
> **Miniature peanut butter cups (optional)**

MIX cream cheese, 1 cup sugar, butter and vanilla with electric mixer on medium speed until well blended. Add flour and baking soda; mix well.

SHAPE dough into equal number of ½-inch and 1-inch diameter balls. Using 1 small and 1 large ball for each snowman, place balls, slightly overlapping, on ungreased cookie sheets. Flatten to ¼-inch thickness with bottom of glass dipped in additional flour. Repeat with remaining balls.

BAKE at 325°F for 19 to 21 minutes or until light golden brown. Cool on wire racks. Sprinkle each snowman with sifted powdered sugar. Decorate with icing as desired. Cut peanut butter cups in half for hats.   ***Makes about 3 dozen cookies***

Shortbread Cookies

Prep Time: 15 minutes   *Bake Time:* 13 minutes

> **1½ cups (3 sticks) butter or margarine, softened**
> **1 package (8 ounces) PHILADELPHIA® Cream Cheese, softened**
> **½ cup granulated sugar**
> **3 cups flour**
> **Powdered sugar**

MIX butter, cream cheese and granulated sugar until well blended. Mix in flour.

SHAPE dough into 1-inch balls; place on ungreased cookie sheets.

BAKE at 400°F for 10 to 13 minutes or until light golden brown and set; cool on wire racks. Sprinkle with powdered sugar.   ***Makes about 6 dozen cookies***

Holiday Cookies: Tint dough with a few drops of food coloring before shaping to add a festive touch.

Holiday Pineapple Cheese Bars

Prep Time: 20 minutes   *Bake Time:* 18 minutes

¼ cup butter *or* margarine
¼ cup packed brown sugar
¾ cup flour
¾ cup finely chopped macadamia nuts
1 can (8 ounces) crushed pineapple, undrained
1 package (8 ounces) PHILADELPHIA® Cream Cheese, softened
¼ cup granulated sugar
1 egg
1 cup BAKER'S® ANGEL FLAKE® Coconut
½ cup coarsely chopped macadamia nuts
1 tablespoon butter or margarine, melted

PREHEAT oven to 350°F.

BEAT ¼ cup butter and brown sugar in small mixing bowl at medium speed with electric mixer until well blended. Add flour and ¾ cup finely chopped nuts; mix well. Press onto bottom of 9-inch square baking pan. Bake 10 minutes. Cool.

DRAIN pineapple, reserving 2 tablespoons liquid.

BEAT cream cheese, reserved liquid, granulated sugar and egg in small mixing bowl at medium speed with electric mixer until well blended. Stir in pineapple. Pour over crust.

SPRINKLE with combined coconut, ½ cup coarsely chopped nuts and 1 tablespoon butter.

BAKE 18 minutes. Cool completely. Cut into bars.

Makes about 1½ dozen bars

Rugelach

Prep Time: 1 hour plus refrigerating   *Bake Time:* 22 minutes

- 1 package (8 ounces) **PHILADELPHIA®** Cream Cheese, softened
- 1¼ cups (2½ sticks) butter *or* margarine, divided
- 2¼ cups flour
- 1 cup finely chopped walnuts *or* pecans
- ½ cup sugar
- 3 teaspoons ground cinnamon, divided
- Raspberry *or* apricot preserves (optional)
- 2 tablespoons sugar

MIX cream cheese and 1 cup of the butter with electric mixer on medium speed until well blended. Gradually add flour, mixing until blended. (Dough will be very soft and sticky.) Divide dough into 4 portions; place each on sheet of plastic wrap. Shape each portion into 1-inch-thick circle, using floured hands. Wrap plastic wrap around each circle to enclose. Refrigerate overnight.

LINE greased cookie sheets with foil or parchment paper. Roll each portion of dough to 11-inch circle on lightly floured surface, lifting dough occasionally to add additional flour to surface to prevent sticking. Melt remaining ¼ cup butter. Mix walnuts, ½ cup sugar and 2 teaspoons of the cinnamon. Brush surface of dough with butter; sprinkle evenly with walnut mixture.

CUT each circle into 16 wedges. Spoon ¼ teaspoon preserves at wide end of each wedge; roll up starting at wide end. Place, point sides down, on prepared cookie sheets. Brush tops lightly with additional melted butter; sprinkle with combined remaining 1 teaspoon cinnamon and 2 tablespoons sugar.

BAKE at 350°F for 19 to 22 minutes or until light golden brown. Remove immediately from cookie sheet. Cool on wire racks.   ***Makes about 5 dozen cookies***

Frosted Pumpkin Squares

Prep Time: 20 minutes   *Bake Time:* 35 minutes

Cake

- ¾ cup (1½ sticks) butter *or* margarine
- 2 cups granulated sugar
- 1 can (16 ounces) pumpkin
- 4 eggs
- 2 cups flour
- 2 teaspoons CALUMET® Baking Powder
- 1 teaspoon ground cinnamon
- ½ teaspoon baking soda
- ½ teaspoon salt
- ¼ teaspoon ground nutmeg
- 1 cup chopped walnuts

Frosting

- 1 package (8 ounces) PHILADELPHIA® Cream Cheese, softened
- ⅓ cup butter *or* margarine
- 1 teaspoon vanilla
- 3 cups sifted powdered sugar

Cake

MIX butter and sugar with electric mixer on medium speed until light and fluffy. Blend in pumpkin and eggs. Mix in combined dry ingredients. Stir in walnuts.

SPREAD into greased and floured 15×10×1-inch baking pan.

BAKE at 350°F for 30 to 35 minutes or until wooden pick inserted in center comes out clean; cool.

Frosting

MIX cream cheese, butter and vanilla in large bowl with electric mixer until creamy. Gradually add sugar, mixing well after each addition. Spread onto cake. Cut into squares.

Makes 2 dozen squares

Cream Cheese Brownies

Prep Time: 15 minutes   *Bake Time:* 40 minutes

4 squares BAKER'S® Unsweetened Baking Chocolate
¾ cup (1½ sticks) butter *or* margarine
2½ cups sugar, divided
5 eggs, divided
1¼ cups flour, divided
1 package (8 ounces) PHILADELPHIA® Cream Cheese, softened

HEAT oven to 350°F. Line 13×9-inch baking pan with foil; grease foil.

MICROWAVE chocolate and butter in large microwavable bowl on HIGH 2 minutes or until butter is melted. Stir until chocolate is completely melted.

STIR 2 cups of the sugar into chocolate mixture until well blended. Mix in 4 of the eggs. Stir in 1 cup of the flour until well blended. Spread in prepared pan. Beat cream cheese, remaining ½ cup sugar, 1 egg and ¼ cup flour in same bowl with wire whisk until well blended. Spoon mixture over brownie batter. Swirl batters with knife to marbleize.

BAKE 40 minutes or until toothpick inserted in center comes out with fudgy crumbs. DO NOT OVERBAKE. Cool in pan on wire rack. Lift out of pan onto cutting board.

Makes 2 dozen

Philadelphia® Apricot Cookies

1½ cups butter *or* margarine, softened
1½ cups granulated sugar
  1 package (8 ounces) PHILADELPHIA® Cream Cheese, softened
  2 eggs
1½ teaspoons grated lemon peel
  2 tablespoons lemon juice
4½ cups all-purpose flour
1½ teaspoons baking powder
    KRAFT® Apricot Preserves
    Powdered sugar

COMBINE butter, granulated sugar and cream cheese in large bowl, mixing until well blended. Blend in eggs, peel and juice. Add combined flour and baking powder; mix well. Cover; refrigerate several hours.

PREHEAT oven to 350°F.

SHAPE level measuring tablespoonfuls of dough into balls. Place on ungreased cookie sheet; flatten slightly. Indent centers; fill with preserves.

BAKE 15 minutes or until lightly browned. Cool on wire rack; sprinkle with powdered sugar.
Makes about 7 dozen cookies

Kringle Cookies

Prep Time: 20 minutes   *Bake Time:* 20 minutes

1½ cups chocolate-covered graham cracker crumbs (about 17 crackers)
  3 tablespoons butter *or* margarine, melted
  1 package (8 ounces) PHILADELPHIA® Cream Cheese, softened
½ cup crunchy peanut butter
  1 cup powdered sugar
  2 squares BAKER'S® Semi-Sweet Chocolate
  1 teaspoon butter *or* margarine

MIX crumbs and melted butter. Press onto bottom of 9-inch square baking pan. Bake at 350°F for 20 minutes. Cool.

BEAT cream cheese, peanut butter and sugar with electric mixer on medium speed until well blended. Spread over crust.

MICROWAVE chocolate with 1 teaspoon butter on HIGH 1 to 2 minutes or until chocolate begins to melt, stirring halfway though heating time. Stir until chocolate is completely melted. Drizzle over cream cheese mixture.

REFRIGERATE 6 hours or overnight. Cut into squares. Store in airtight container in refrigerator.
Makes 18 servings

Lemon Nut Bars

Prep Time: 30 minutes   *Bake Time:* 40 minutes

1⅓ cups all-purpose flour
½ cup firmly packed brown sugar
¼ cup granulated sugar
¾ cup butter or margarine
1 cup old-fashioned or quick oats, uncooked
½ cup chopped nuts
1 package (8 ounces) PHILADELPHIA® Cream Cheese, softened
1 egg
1 tablespoon grated lemon peel
3 tablespoons lemon juice

PREHEAT oven to 350°F.

STIR together flour and sugars in medium bowl. Cut in butter until mixture resembles coarse crumbs. Stir in oats and nuts. Reserve 1 cup crumb mixture; press remaining crumb mixture onto bottom of greased 13×9-inch baking pan. Bake 15 minutes.

BEAT cream cheese, egg, lemon peel and juice in small mixing bowl at medium speed with electric mixer until well blended. Pour over crust; sprinkle with reserved crumb mixture.

BAKE 25 minutes. Cool in pan on wire rack. Cut into bars.

Makes about 3 dozen bars

Philadelphia® Cheesecake Brownies

Prep Time: 20 minutes   *Bake Time:* 40 minutes

- 1 package (19.8 ounces) brownie mix (do not use mix that includes syrup pouch)
- 1 package (8 ounces) PHILADELPHIA® Cream Cheese, softened
- ⅓ cup sugar
- 1 egg
- ½ teaspoon vanilla

PREPARE brownie mix as directed on package. Pour into greased 13×9-inch baking pan.

BEAT cream cheese with electric mixer on medium speed until smooth. Mix in sugar until blended. Add egg and vanilla; mix just until blended. Pour cream cheese mixture over brownie batter; cut through batter with knife several times for marble effect.

BAKE at 350°F for 35 to 40 minutes or until cream cheese mixture is lightly browned. Cool. Cut into squares.   *Makes 2 dozen*

Special Extras: For extra chocolate flavor, sprinkle 1 cup BAKER'S® Semi-Sweet Real Chocolate Chips over top of brownies before baking.

Tip: For 13×9-inch glass baking dish, bake at 325°F.

Tip

To save cleanup time, line baking pans with foil, leaving several inches of foil overhanging each end. Grease the foil if the recipe calls for a greased pan. Once the cookies or brownies have baked and cooled, use the foil to remove them from the pan before cutting into bars.

Philadelphia® Cheesecake Brownies

Index

Index

METRIC CONVERSION CHART

VOLUME MEASUREMENTS (dry)

$1/8$ teaspoon = 0.5 mL
$1/4$ teaspoon = 1 mL
$1/2$ teaspoon = 2 mL
$3/4$ teaspoon = 4 mL
1 teaspoon = 5 mL
1 tablespoon = 15 mL
2 tablespoons = 30 mL
$1/4$ cup = 60 mL
$1/3$ cup = 75 mL
$1/2$ cup = 125 mL
$2/3$ cup = 150 mL
$3/4$ cup = 175 mL
1 cup = 250 mL
2 cups = 1 pint = 500 mL
3 cups = 750 mL
4 cups = 1 quart = 1 L

VOLUME MEASUREMENTS (fluid)

1 fluid ounce (2 tablespoons) = 30 mL
4 fluid ounces ($1/2$ cup) = 125 mL
8 fluid ounces (1 cup) = 250 mL
12 fluid ounces ($1 1/2$ cups) = 375 mL
16 fluid ounces (2 cups) = 500 mL

WEIGHTS (mass)

$1/2$ ounce = 15 g
1 ounce = 30 g
3 ounces = 90 g
4 ounces = 120 g
8 ounces = 225 g
10 ounces = 285 g
12 ounces = 360 g
16 ounces = 1 pound = 450 g

DIMENSIONS

$1/16$ inch = 2 mm
$1/8$ inch = 3 mm
$1/4$ inch = 6 mm
$1/2$ inch = 1.5 cm
$3/4$ inch = 2 cm
1 inch = 2.5 cm

OVEN TEMPERATURES

250°F = 120°C
275°F = 140°C
300°F = 150°C
325°F = 160°C
350°F = 180°C
375°F = 190°C
400°F = 200°C
425°F = 220°C
450°F = 230°C

BAKING PAN SIZES

Utensil	Size in Inches/Quarts	Metric Volume	Size in Centimeters
Baking or Cake Pan (square or rectangular)	8×8×2	2 L	20×20×5
	9×9×2	2.5 L	23×23×5
	12×8×2	3 L	30×20×5
	13×9×2	3.5 L	33×23×5
Loaf Pan	8×4×3	1.5 L	20×10×7
	9×5×3	2 L	23×13×7
Round Layer Cake Pan	8×1½	1.2 L	20×4
	9×1½	1.5 L	23×4
Pie Plate	8×1¼	750 mL	20×3
	9×1¼	1 L	23×3
Baking Dish or Casserole	1 quart	1 L	—
	1½ quart	1.5 L	—
	2 quart	2 L	—